Great Meetings!
great results

To Order More Copies

To order more copies of *Great Meetings! Great Results* please contact us using the information below. We welcome inquiries about our wholesale rates and quantity discounts.

mailing address:	Great Meetings! Inc., P.O. Box 3883, Portland, Maine, 04104-3883, U.S.A.
website address:	www.greatmeetingsinc.com
e-mail address:	info@greatmeetingsinc.com
phone/fax:	(207) 773-0487
toll free:	(888) 374-6010 (in Canada and the U.S.)

Training and Consultation

Great Meetings! Inc. offers customized training and consultation for businesses and organizations. For more information, please contact us at the address above.

High Praise for

Great Meetings! Great Results

"Great Meetings! Great Results properly describes what Pam Plumb and Dee Kelsey promise in this very practical and useful book. I admire both the comprehensive scope of their teaching and the detail of real life situations. If you want to lead people with great facilitation, read this book and keep it near you for quick reference."

Tom Chappell, President and CEO
Tom's of Maine, Kennebunk, ME

"Great Meetings! has been the book I've recommended to others since it was published — and it just got better. The new edition has expanded content, more incisive graphics, and lots of insight. Get, read and re-read this book. Become a better facilitator."

Geoff Ball, President
SmartGroups™, Los Altos, CA

"For facilitators and mediators who work with larger groups, *Great Meetings! Great Results* is a treasure trove of information in a format that is easy to use. For people who think they are too busy to expand the tools they use in problem-solving groups, this is a must resource."

Dr. Margaret S. Herrman, Senior Associate and Director
Dispute Resolution Services
Carl Vinson Institute of Government, University of Georgia, Athens, GA

"Dee Kelsey and Pam Plumb have identified the essentials to facilitate not just an effective meeting but a 'great meeting!' They put it into easily understandable terms that prove to be comprehensive for any scenario. For those of us whose working life depends on quality engagement and visible outcomes from meetings, this guide is practical, accessible, and relevant."

Don Borut, Executive Director
National League of Cities, Washington, D.C.

"People everywhere dread meetings, but this book, with its practical, proven tips and techniques has delivered great results for me with groups in London, Belgrade, San Juan, Winnipeg, Washington, and even at my own family reunion. *Great Meetings! Great Results* outlines practical and proven steps for group process that leads to solid results. Read this book and the next time someone labels you a 'process person' you can feel proud."

Peter Twichell, Director of Program Development
YouthBuild U.S.A., Boston, MA

"This is the book I turn to first when I am looking for approaches to a meeting. It is well worth sitting down with this book before, during and after each facilitation. I am delighted with the new edition. Kelsey and Plumb have added new ideas and techniques, as well as tools. It is even clearer than the last edition. I would not have thought that possible."

Zena Zumeta, Mediator, Facilitator, Trainer
Mediation Training & Consultation Institute, Ann Arbor, MI

"Bravo, Bravo, Bravo! *Great Meetings! Great Results* is even better than the first great edition. It's an elegant guide to meeting facilitation. This book is an essential resource for every meeting planner's tool box."

Dr. Bruce Wolford, Director of the Research and Service Center
Eastern Kentucky University, Richmond, KY

"This book models everything a good meeting should be — straightforward, well organized, current, accessible to a diverse audience and a good use of time that yields better results. This book is an excellent guide to leveraging the time, money, relationships and results of the different types of a meeting that form the daily operations of business."

Katherine Greenleaf, Senior Vice President
Wright Express L.L.C., South Portland, ME

"I found excellent tools throughout the book. For example, the brainstorming examples in Chapter 6 are very clear and helpful; the long range planning process model very effective and easy to follow. Overall, the content of *Great Meetings! Great Results* is well written, easy to use and a great resource for all kinds of facilitation needs."

Jean Whitney, Corporate Education and Training
Banknorth N.A., Portland, ME

Great Meetings!

great results

A practical guide for facilitating
successful, productive meetings

by Dee Kelsey and Pam Plumb

Hanson Park Press
Great Meetings! Inc.
Portland, Maine

Great Meetings! Great Results
by Dee Kelsey and Pam Plumb
Copyright © 2004 Great Meetings! Inc.

Published by Great Meetings! Inc.
P.O. Box 3883, Portland, Maine, 04104-3883.

Cover and page design by Jennifer Ellis.
Illustrations by Beth Braganca.
Illustrations in chapter 11 by Kippy Rudy are indicated by the KR symbol.

First printing, July 2004
Second printing, January 2006
Manufactured in the United States

ISBN 0-9658354-1-3

Library of Congress Control Number: 200419884

Great Meetings!

great results

Acknowledgements

THE REWRITING AND EXPANSION OF *GREAT MEETINGS! HOW TO FACILITATE LIKE A PRO* AND its transformation into *Great Meetings! Great Results* is the result of our own continued learning from the practice of and training in facilitation. Our thinking has continued to evolve; we have developed new ideas and others have shared their good ideas with us. We owe a great debt to our many clients and colleagues who have inspired and challenged us and given us new insights about meeting management and facilitation. Their feedback and encouragement have been invaluable.

Many friends and colleagues helped talk us through the development of this next generation of *Great Meetings!* To each and everyone who has lent us a hand, we are grateful. We owe special thanks to Mary Lou Michael, who guided us gracefully through the daunting task of facilitating our visioning and long range planning for Great Meetings! Inc. We are grateful for her patience, skill and support.

Once again Jennifer Ellis, our editor and designer, has brought our text alive on the pages of *Great Meetings! Great Results* and given it a great new look. She is a pleasure to work with and we value her considerable professional skills. We would also like to thank Kippy Rudy whose drawings from the first edition continue to be a lively part of the new book and Beth Braganca, who has added wonderful new illustrations that help to make the book engaging and interesting.

Finally, we thank those supportive souls on our respective home fronts, Emily Kelsey, now a busy seventh grader, and Peter Plumb, who would rather be sailing than birthing a new book and business. They have generously tolerated us through endless hours spent on this new adventure. Bless you both.

Great Meetings!

great results

Table of Contents

Great Meetings!

great results

Introduction

GREAT MEETINGS! GREAT RESULTS IS ABOUT GENERATING GREAT IDEAS, SAVING TIME AND getting results from your meetings. The book is designed to provide a practical guide for people who are interested in making every one of their meetings more productive, creative, effective and fun. It is based on the belief that groups of people can generate better decisions than any one of us might come up with alone. The members of a group will provide different insights, bring unique experiences and expertise to bear on the problem and feed on each others' ideas to build a synergy, a whole which is greater than the mere mathematical sum of the parts

This book is not a scholarly dissertation, but a "how to" book built from years of practical experience. In 1997 we published *Great Meetings! How to Facilitate Like a Pro* based on our experience facilitating and teaching facilitation. We have been delight-ed with the success of the book and trust it has led to many more well run, productive meetings. Seven years later, we have expanded and updated *Great Meetings!* and changed the book's title to *Great Meetings! Great Results* to reflect our belief that not everyone cares about being a pro at facilitating, but everyone does want great results from meetings they lead or attend.

It takes skill to work as a group. Meetings take planning and preparation to be successful. Agendas need to be designed carefully to meet the needs of the situation. Managing a meeting takes a host of facilitation skills and a full bag of process tools. This book is designed to help you understand the various preparation and design steps that will assist you in planning effective meetings and to give you a wide variety of facilitation tools and techniques for managing meetings well.

What's Inside the Book?

CHAPTER ONE: FACILITATION: THE KEY TO A GREAT MEETING clarifies what facilitation is, distinguishing it from meeting organization, process design, process coaching, and organizational development consulting. You will find a description of the facilitator's role and a discussion of how to manage the multiple roles you may need to play in a meeting. In addition, we identify the attitudes that support good facilitation and the tool kit a good facilitator will need.

CHAPTER TWO: KNOWING YOUR GROUP focuses on group dynamics. It is not a thorough study of this complex subject, but an overview of how groups work and develop. Its purpose is to build your awareness of the complexities of groups as you plan for and facilitate meetings. The chapter covers factors in group dynamics, stages of group development, behaviors and roles that affect the functioning of groups, and overt and covert group issues.

CHAPTER THREE: GETTING A GOOD START guides you through the steps of preparing for a meeting, including deciding whether or not a meeting is even necessary. It outlines how to assess the purpose and desired outcomes of the meeting and how to gather relevant background information. The chapter concludes with a meeting preparation checklist.

CHAPTER FOUR: DESIGNING A GREAT MEETING gives you guidance in effective meeting design, including the key steps for getting the meeting off to a good start and concluding it to ensure results and follow through. You will find ideas for how to handle the logistics of a meeting and suggestions for room arrangements.

CHAPTER FIVE: UNDERSTANDING PROCESS outlines three basic process steps: analysis of the issue or problem, envisioning or identifying the goal, and decision making, which includes generating and evaluating options. The chapter suggests helpful tools to use in each of those steps. It provides tips on long range planning processes and identifies several specialized meeting methods and where to find out more about them.

CHAPTER SIX: CHOOSING THE RIGHT TOOL provides a broad selection of tools to use for generating ideas, evaluating ideas and coming to a decision. Each tool's description will let you know when the tool is most helpful and how to use it.

CHAPTER SEVEN: MAXIMIZING YOUR GROUP'S POTENTIAL outlines a number of process techniques to help your group work at its highest potential. It includes warm up techniques for group forming, methods for generating discussion and techniques for keeping groups on track.

CHAPTER EIGHT: PROMOTING POSITIVE COMMUNICATION deals with the communications skills, which are critical both to your effectiveness as a facilitator and to the participants' ability to have a successful meeting. This discussion includes establishing a good communication environment, listening skills, "I" messages, different types of questioning, and ways to reframe language.

CHAPTER NINE: MANAGING CONFLICT IN GROUPS addresses conflict in groups. Differences in opinion are positive and helpful to a group. This chapter helps you manage the negative side of conflict and encourage the creativity of differences. It begins with ways to prevent unnecessary conflict and an explanation of the sources of conflict, and then offers methods for intervening in group conflicts and addressing interpersonal conflicts that arise in group.

CHAPTER TEN: INTERVENTIONS: WHEN TO STEP IN discusses methods for intervening in challenging group situations or with difficult individual behaviors. We offer a method for analyzing the nature of the problem and choosing the appropriate approach for intervening including how to interrupt a person when necessary. Included are case studies to demonstrate this process in action.

CHAPTER ELEVEN: INTEGRATING GRAPHICS INTO YOUR MEETINGS Meetings introduces you to the basics of using graphics to enhance your facilitation. It gives you ideas for graphic methods to help organize a group's thinking and graphic tools. It includes a number of graphic symbols and formats to add to your tool kit.

CHAPTER TWELVE: REFLECTIONS ON THE ART OF FACILITATION gives you an opportunity to look at personal issues that affect your ability as a facilitator. It invites you to reflect on what is likely to get in your way of being successful and what you can do to stay as grounded and effective as possible. There is a discussion of how to define success for yourself as a facilitator. And finally, it raises some critical ethical questions that relate to facilitation.

How Can You Use This Book?

There are several ways you can use this book. You can read it from cover to cover, gain a new understanding about how to prepare and facilitate effective meetings and then put it away. We hope, however, that you will keep the book handy and use it as a regular reference. When you have a meeting coming up, you can use the preparation checklist to remind yourself to ask all the necessary questions before you start to design the meeting. You can use the agenda planning model to help outline your agenda or check the process steps and the chapter on tools to find the most appropriate tool for your meeting. Once you have planned your agenda and picked the appropriate tools, you can copy the tool and take it with you to the meeting. You might want to copy your back up tool ideas as well. If you hit a stumbling block in a group, you can turn to the book for some ideas on how to get moving again. Our hope is that your book will become dog-eared from frequent use.

> We hope your book will become dog-eared from use.

Great Meetings!Great Results is designed to be useful for those of you just starting out in facilitation as well as those who are already experienced and are looking for new insights and tools of the trade. Hopefully, each of you will take from the book the level of information you need.

The facilitation material in *Great Meetings!Great Results* is not designed for just one venue, such as corporate teams, non-profit boards or public meetings. Wherever you are using your facilitation skills, the basic tenets of the material should serve you well. Every situation has its own special needs and you will have to take those needs into account each time you plan and facilitate a meeting.

Because of the breadth of applications for *Great Meetings!Great Results*, when we use the word "client" we intend it to be understood very broadly as whoever is asking you to facilitate: yourself, your supervisor, a co-worker or a paying client. Also, on the subject of language, we use the terms extrovert and introvert as defined in the Myers Briggs Personality Type Indicators, meaning that an extrovert is likely to process ideas by talking them through while an introvert is likely to process ideas internally first. We also struggled with how to use personal pronouns in this book in regard to gender. We have no intention to have you picture facilitators as the sole province of either men or women, but find using he/she everywhere to be tiresome. Our solution is to alternate gender pronouns by chapter.

Crediting Sources

The field of facilitation has been growing rapidly. Tools and techniques have been traded around over and over again, growing and changing with various evolutions along the way and often obscuring the actual originator of the technique. Where we know the originator, we have acknowledged that ownership, but in most instances we simply don't know who it is. We always welcome information from our readers that will help us identify the original sources and will add these credits in future editions.

The book has a variety of tool descriptions, which can be copied and used repeatedly. Please feel free to do so. But we ask that you acknowledge the source and use integrity in distinguishing between copying small sections and expropriating the whole book.

We welcome any suggestions you have for improving our book. Please send your suggestions, comments or book orders to Great Meetings! Inc., P.O. Box 3883, Portland, ME 04104-3883.

You can also contact us by e-mail at info@greatmeetingsinc.com or call us toll free at 1-888-374-6010 or 207-773-0487.

Great Meetings!

great results

Chapter One

Facilitation: The Key to a Great Meeting

FACILITATION IS THE PROCESS OF HELPING A GROUP COMPLETE A TASK, SOLVE A PROBLEM or come to agreement to the mutual satisfaction of the participants. Successful facilitation takes preparation and planning, a constructive attitude, certain skills and behaviors, and a collection of process tools.

A facilitator may be an outside, independent person without a stake in the results of the meeting. Or she may be the leader or a member of the group with a real interest in the meeting's outcome. In either case, the facilitator's job is to serve the group, not to dominate it. The facilitator impacts and guides the process but does not give input on the content of a meeting — that comes from the participants. One measure of good facilitation is that the group members feel they've done their work themselves.

People often have multiple roles in a meeting. For managing multiple roles, see the sections in this chapter on "Clarifying your Role as a Facilitator," and "Balancing the Dual Roles of Facilitator and Group Leader/Member."

Even if you are a participant as well as facilitator in your meeting, you function neutrally when you facilitate. If you are working as an outside consultant, the facilitator's role is different from that of many other consultants in that your job is to give process advice, rather than content advice.

> One measure of good facilitation is that the group members feel they've done the work themselves.

If you were to look at a continuum of roles from meeting planner to organizational development consultant, the facilitator would fall somewhere in the middle. When you are facilitating, you are doing much more than just setting up the logistics of a meeting. You are making assessments about the needs of the group and providing advice on the best design for the meeting and the best tools and techniques for accomplishing the tasks. You are being very attentive to the needs of the group as a whole, as well as to individuals within the group. Your role, however, is focused on the group's needs to accomplish its task. You are not the specialist called in to diagnose organizational problems and recommend changes. Nor are you guiding the growth and development of group members.

The Place of Facilitation in a Spectrum of Group Activities

Groups have different kinds of support and service needs. It is important to understand the distinction between these needs so that you can assess whether you are the right person for the job, both in terms of your interest and your skills. The chart below outlines some of the services groups require, as well as the role and body of knowledge required to provide that service. In this book, our focus is only on facilitation. The more complex roles require additional training and expertise.

Service	Role	Expertise
Meeting Organizer	• Schedule and organize the logistics of a meeting	• Understanding of space requirements, schedules, equipment, refreshments, room set-up
Facilitator	• Prepare and facilitate a meeting	• Assessment, meeting design, process tools, facilitative behaviors and skills, group dynamics, conflict management, graphics, communication skills
Complex Process Designer	• Design steps in a multiple meeting process involving a variety of stakeholders	• Same as facilitator, plus information gathering, stakeholder analysis
Process Coach	• Observe a group and give feedback regarding their process and interaction	• Understanding of interpersonal and group dynamics, meeting design management
Organizational Development Consultant	• Diagnose, analyze, intervene, give feedback on organizational systems; guide personal growth and understanding in the context of a group	• Understanding of intrapersonal, interpersonal and systems dynamics

Facilitative Attitudes

An effective facilitator has to have respect for all group members, expecting and fostering the best in participants by modeling and affirming positive behavior. Facilitators also need the skills to be assertive, to intervene when necessary to protect group members from attack, to name a conflict when it has emerged, and to bring the group back on focus. A calm presence, flexibility, creativity and a sense of humor will go a long way to support any group and its process.

The following are attitudes that underlie quality facilitation work. They are simple to understand, but for many of us will require a lifetime of practice to adopt fully.

> **What would serve the group best right now?**

SERVANT OF THE GROUP AND ITS PROCESS: The facilitator's role is to support the group's work on its task. Process, prevention and intervention decisions are always prefaced by asking yourself, "What would serve the group best right now?"

RESPECT AND COMPASSION: The facilitator is best able to serve the group if she can truly feel respect and compassion for the individuals within the group as well as for the group as a whole. This is not the same as personal fondness. It means respecting intentions, always listening for understanding out of a belief that everyone has something to offer which is worth understanding, and having compassion for the challenge of working in groups as well as the problem at hand.

POSITIVE: It is important to trust that groups can work effectively and to encourage the group — especially when it gets bogged down. Always be constructive in your own comments and attitude.

FLEXIBLE: Have an extensive tool kit of process techniques and be willing to change processes if necessary. Be a process advocate and educator, but also be willing to let go of a process if it doesn't work and try something else.

NON-DEFENSIVE: When someone in the group attacks or challenges you, don't argue back. Stay centered and focus on their concerns. Defending yourself just adds a complicating dynamic to an already complicated situation and focuses attention on you rather than the issue at hand. Anger directed toward you is often displaced anger or frustration about the group.

> Be an advocate for good process, not for content, and put your own opinions aside.

NEUTRAL: Being neutral does not mean being passive; it means remaining non-judgmental of the group's content. As a facilitator, be an advocate for good process, not for content, and put your own opinions aside. Remember, the group must define and solve its own issues, and even if you have a brilliant solution for them, they won't own it, believe in it or be willing to implement it if it isn't theirs. If you are facilitating a group of which you are also a participant and have opinions on the content, save them until you resume the role of participant. For a more in-depth explanation of managing multiple roles, see the sections in this chapter on "Clarifying your Role as a Facilitator," and "Balancing the Dual Roles of Facilitator and Group Leader/Member."

The Facilitator's Job Description:

- Help clarify the purpose and outcomes of a meeting
- Plan and design the meeting
- Build a good foundation in the meeting opening
- Support good communication and full participation
- Keep the meeting on track, encouraging and affirming good process
- Listen intently at multiple levels, reflecting back and clarifying
- Guide the group through conflicts and other difficult situations
- Manage and adapt process, making process suggestions as necessary
- Stay neutral on content while facilitating
- Serve the whole group

The Facilitator's Kit of Essential Skills

LISTENING SKILLS: A facilitator needs to listen intently to thoroughly under-stand each person and the group as a whole. It is important to listen on many levels such as: the content, emotion, subtext and intention. A facilitator listens to the group as a whole, looking for areas of agreement or disagreement, sensing when the group is confused. Listening includes using your eyes to read and understand body language and visual clues. See the section on Listening Skills on page 151 of *Chapter Eight: Promoting Positive Communication.*

SUMMARIZING AND CLARIFYING SKILLS: A facilitator should be able to summa-rize an individual's comments, capturing the kernel of what the person wants to add to the discussion or to summarize the accomplishments and agreements of the group at the end of the meeting. It is important to be able to clarify the dis-tinctions between two points of view in the group or the choices facing the group.

GROUP DEVELOPMENT/DYNAMICS SKILLS: Group development skills: a facilitator should have an awareness of group development and group dynamics. There are many factors here to be aware of, including the group's history, size of the group, formality or informality, task or social orientation, stage of group development, etc.

PROCESS SKILLS: A facilitator needs to know a variety of process tools and techniques and how to choose the most effective ones for a given group or situation. It is important to understand where the group is in the process steps and whether it needs a tool to generate, evaluate or decide on ideas.

INTERVENTION/CONFLICT MANAGEMENT SKILLS: A facilitator needs to know when and how to step in if something is interfering with the group's work, whether that is the behavior of an individual or a group situation, in a way that keeps the group on track and honors individuals. Similarly, a facilitator needs to encourage the differences of opinion, which help the group generate new ideas or evaluate ideas from different perspectives and, at the same time, mitigate emotionally charged, personalized conflict.

RECORDING AND GRAPHIC SKILLS: A facilitator needs to be able to record a group's work in a manner that helps the group follow, remember and clarify its thinking. The methods may include flipchart sheets, overheads or computer screens. Whether the facilitator records herself or assigns that task to a different group member, the goal is the same — to support the group's work.

Clarifying Your Role as a Facilitator

At the outset of a meeting it is extremely important that all involved be clear about their roles. The group members should know what is expected of them, as should the chair or leader of the group. As the designated facilitator, it is possible to play one or more of the following roles.

FACILITATOR: This means you are serving the group by guiding the process of the meetings: helping with the flow of discussion; working to get full participation; keeping the group moving towards its goal, etc. While you should have general familiarity with the content of the meeting (i.e. be content-literate), you do not have to be a content expert and you will not be contributing to the content of the meeting.

FACILITATOR/EXPERT: If you have content expertise, you may be asked to both facilitate a group and offer your advice about the content the group is considering. For example, if you are a marketing specialist and are facilitating a group which needs to make decisions about marketing a new product, you might be asked to give your opinion about what marketing strategy will work best. However, in the role of facilitator/expert, you don't have a stake in the outcome of the group's work.

FACILITATOR/LEADER: If you are the leader of the group, you have responsibility for the ultimate outcomes and success of the group overall and, therefore, a big stake in the outcome of the group's work. In addition, if you supervise the members of the group, that will add a challenging dynamic to the meeting. See the sections on "Balancing the Dual Roles of Facilitator and Group Leader/Member," on page 16 of this chapter. There is an inevitable dynamic that the power differential will impact on the group, often making it harder for participants to speak freely or take risks. Therefore, you must either judge carefully whether the group can overcome this dynamic or relinquish the role of facilitator.

FACILITATOR/MEMBER: This dual role implies that you have a stake in the product of the group as well as the process of the group—you care about what the group accomplishes as well as how it accomplishes it. As a group member you will want to be able to give your opinion during the meeting. As the facilitator you will want to ensure that a high quality process is followed. Beware: It is challenging to play the dual role well! See the section on "Balancing the Dual Roles of Facilitator and Group Leader/Member" on the following pages.

RECORDER: As the recorder you are responsible for writing down any output of the group onto flipcharts or other graphic technologies. In other words, you are creating a visual group memory. This requires excellent listening and summarizing skills, as well as a good graphics ability. Some groups assume that the person playing this role is also responsible for getting the materials typed and distributed. Clarify explicitly who is expected to write up and distribute notes after the meeting.

TIME KEEPER: The time keeper is responsible for keeping an eye on the clock and the time limits agreed upon for each item on the agenda. This role can be played by the facilitator or by someone else.

BREAK MONITOR: The break monitor's role is to remind the facilitator when it is time for a break or a stretch.

Sometime before the meeting gets underway, you should discuss with the group the role you intend to play and check for agreement. It can be helpful to give away roles such as time keeper, break monitor or recorder, both to make your job easier and to get the group members more involved in the ownership of the meeting.

Balancing the Dual Roles of Facilitator and Group Leader/Member

Often, the facilitator is described as a person with no stake in the outcome of a group's decision making, a person who is present only to guide the process. However, we are often called on to be facilitators for groups that we also lead or participate in, therefore giving us a vested interest in the product of the meeting. It is tricky, but possible to play these dual roles effectively. Below are some guidelines to make it easier.

1. Define clearly to the group what roles you will be playing by naming them. For example: "Today I am going to facilitate this meeting — that is, keep us on track with the agenda and suggest some ways we might go about making a decision. As a member of this unit, I also want a chance to add my opinions to the group discussion. I will let you know when I am switching from being the facilitator to being a participant."

2. Notify the group when you are switching roles. For example: "Could someone else facilitate for awhile? I'd like to step out of my role as facilitator and  give my opinion about this topic." Then, "Thanks for facilitating, Tasha, I can move back into that role now." Or, more informally, "As a participant, I want to share my opinion on the subject." Picture yourself as having different hats, a facilitator hat and a participant hat. Tell the group when you are changing hats. You can only wear one hat at a time to facilitate effectively.

3. Encourage participation from everyone present (not just those who agree with you), check the accuracy of your summaries, and use an agreed-upon decision making method. Ask the group to help you in facilitating in a fair and balanced way, and to tell you when you are not.

4. There is a risk that the facilitator will be perceived to be using process to move the group to her desired outcome. Watch for little actions that would give a perception that you are not neutral. Remember not to praise one person's suggestion while not praising others. In a brainstorming session, write up all ideas, not just the ones you agree with. A danger of playing dual roles is that you unconsciously (or consciously) can choose a process that will lead to the outcome you desire.

> **Watch for little actions that would give a perception that you are not neutral.**

5. Hold your own opinions until others have spoken. If your ideas have already been said by others, don't repeat them.

Keep open the option of bringing in a professional facilitator or someone from another department or group. If you or other group members have strong opinions about the outcome of a particular discussion, or strong feelings about some of the participants, give yourself permission to bring in an outside facilitator or ask someone else in the group to facilitate. This will free you up to put your energy on the content of the meeting. It is a sign of wisdom, not weakness, to let someone else facilitate in these circumstances and may save time and expense down the road. If your organization trains everyone in facilitation skills, you will have lots of able facilitators to choose from.

> **It is a sign of wisdom, not weakness, to let someone else facilitate in certain circumstances.**

Great Meetings!

great results

Chapter Two
Knowing Your Group

BOOKS HAVE BEEN WRITTEN ON THE SUBJECTS OF GROUP DYNAMICS, GROUP DEVELOP-
ment and group process. In this chapter we are not trying to reproduce such in-
depth work. Rather our goal is to focus on the group dynamics and group development issues which you will want to consider as you design and implement processes
for facilitation.

Group Dynamics

Any time a group of people comes together to work there are dynamics at play.
External forces (norms, organizational culture, etc.), the history of the group, sub-
groupings and individual members, membership within the group, group norms, the
size of the group and informal and formal leadership within the group are just some

of those dynamics. You should know enough about the group to facilitate effectively. It's the "enough" that's the tricky part. If your only role is facilitator of a simple process, don't worry about knowing everything about past history and group dynamics. Just make sure you know about any major events in the history of the group — positive or negative — that may impact this facilitation. Too much knowledge may even work against your effectiveness. Your role is to serve the group now and to guide and model effective process.

> Even if you are very
>
> familiar with the
>
> group, try to look
>
> with fresh eyes to
>
> find new ways to
>
> help the group
>
> work well.

If you are a member of the group, you may already know a great deal about the group's history and norms. It is still important to take time to consider the impact of the group's dynamics (including your part in those dynamics) on its ability to work effectively together and on your meeting design. Even if you are very familiar with the group, try to look with fresh eyes to find new ways to help the group work well.

On the following pages are some of the factors in group dynamics and possible implications for the facilitator. This list should be used along with the meeting preparation checklist in *Chapter Three: Getting a Good Start.*

Factors in Group Dynamics	Possible Implications and/or Interventions for Facilitation
EXTERNAL FORCES: Norms, expectations, assumptions, culture of, or scrutiny by the larger organization, the public, etc.	• Acknowledge and discuss impact on the group. • May affect ground rules.
HISTORY: Of the group or task	• Acknowledge it. • If the history needs to be overcome, structure activities that will help the group move forward.
Of individuals	• Ignore unless it brings value to or interferes with the group. • Acknowledge impact (positive or negative) of past leaders and members. • Get agreement that people will leave "baggage" behind.
GROUP NORMS:	• Norms in a group are often unspoken. Establishing ground rules encourages discussion about which norms are desired.
SIZE OF GROUP:	• Smaller groups can often be facilitated informally. Larger groups need more formal procedures. • Often people monitor their own behavior more responsibly in a small group than in a large one. • Be honest with yourself about your own comfort and skill level with small vs. large groups.

Factors in Group Dynamics	Possible Implications and/or Interventions for Facilitation
MEMBERSHIP:	
Old/new members	• Integrate new members into the group. Acknowledge contribution of old members.
Willingness to be members	• Determine what resistant members need to participate fully.
Changing membership	• Establish ground rules re: staying fully informed, revisiting decisions, etc.
Sub-groupings	• Acknowledge them. • Encourage dialogue between groups. • Use exercises that mix groups.
LEADERSHIP:	
Formal/informal	• Acknowledge and clarify the role of the formal leader. • Actively involve informal leaders; however, don't let them take the meeting in an inappropriate direction.
OTHER FACTORS:	
Voluntary versus mandated participation	• Acknowledge; ask what members need to participate fully.
Volunteer versus paid work	• Surface and address expectations volunteers may have regarding compensation (recognition, develop new skills, friendships, etc.)
Longevity in workplace, gender, age, individual agendas, etc.	• Listen for ways these factors may impact effectiveness of group. • Address when factors impact the group's work or cohesion.

Group Development

All groups go through stages of development. The amount of time and intensity of each stage will depend on the group, its dynamics, its task and the amount of time it has. Groups develop in a variety of ways. While some progress through each stage in order, others skip stages and need to come back to them later. As external and internal factors cause change in the group and/or its task (new members join and old leave; crisis or change of direction in the organization, etc.), the group is likely to revisit earlier stages of development. It is possible for a group to get stuck in one stage — particularly storming — and never progress. However, with good facilitation, you can mirror back to the group where the group seems to be stuck, and help them move forward.

In his article, "Developmental Sequence in Small Groups" (Psychological Bulletin 63, vi, 1965), Bruce Tuckman proposes his four stage model for group development: forming, storming, norming and performing.

Forming: This characterizes the time when a group is first coming together, or when new members are joining the group. Some have referred to this as the "ritual sniffing" phase. Group members are concerned about inclusion: whether and how they belong and how safe it is to be part of this group. Therefore, this stage is characterized by politeness, low conflict and superficial disclosure. The group often looks to the facilitator or leader for strong direction.

FACILITATOR'S TASK: The task of the facilitator in this stage is to assess what group forming work needs to be done, and then to structure an appropriate opening so that people can feel safe, legitimized, valued and have a sanctioned way to get a feel for one another. Forming can be accomplished through a process of:

- planning introductions and orientation
- reviewing the "road map" (desired outcomes and agenda)
- using warm up activities

- inviting expressions of expectations
- establishing ground rules
- agreeing upon decision-making methods

WHEN THE FACILITATOR IS NEW TO AN EXISTING GROUP: An interesting twist to the forming stage occurs when the facilitator is new to a group which has its own history and culture. In this instance, you need to draw the group back to the forming stage just long enough for the group to get to know you and feel comfortable with your facilitating. Beware of doing too much forming for your sake (i.e. long introductions of each person); you may lose the group. Ideally, you will have done some of this work prior to the start of the first meeting by meeting group members, conducting an email survey, etc.

Storming: Storming is the stage where members are concerned about control, power and influence. It often manifests through disagreements about process, emotional responses to task demands, and challenges to the facilitator or leader.

FACILITATOR'S TASK: The task of the facilitator in this stage is to assess and name the specific storming issues of the group, and guide and model good conflict resolution process.

- remember you are not the target
- serve as a mirror to the group
- separate the problem from the person
- acknowledge, then deal with or defer any concerns. See *Chapter Ten: Interventions: When to Step In* for a detailed discussion of this.
- enforce the ground rules
- be assertive in your role as process expert

Note: Not every conflict is an indication of storming. Healthy conflict over content and process can occur at every stage of group development. See *Chapter Nine: Managing Conflict in Groups* for a detailed discussion.

Norming: Norming is the stage in which group members move toward inter-dependence. Individually, group members are focused on building caring and a sense of belonging in the group.

FACILITATOR'S TASK: The task of the facilitator is to support the group's func-tioning:

- mirror and record norms that are emerging
- affirm the group's cohesiveness and the work it has taken to get there
- affirm the positive value of expressing differences
- guide the group through collaborative negotiation
- provide opportunities for the group to enjoy its connectedness

Performing: Performing is the stage where the group is working collabora-tively and is highly productive. To an outsider, the group might appear to be only task focused, but the strong underpinnings of trust, respect, shared norms and overarching goals are in place.

FACILITATOR'S TASK: The task of the facilitator at this stage is:

- offer effective processes for getting the task accomplished
- format the work in a way that is useful to the group
- affirm the good work of the group
- stay out of the way when not needed

Behaviors and Roles That Affect the Functioning of Groups

Behaviors in groups can be categorized by whether they: 1. help accomplish the group task (task-oriented); 2. help maintain good relationships among members (socially-oriented); or 3. hinder the group by expressing individual needs or goals unrelated to the group's purposes (self-oriented).

As a facilitator, it is important to know what behaviors to support and encourage in groups. You want to encourage the expression of both task- and social-related roles, and to maintain a balance of the two as necessary. Of course, you want to discourage self-oriented behaviors as much as possible, and intervene if they are distracting or draining the group.

We each behave in a way that reflects our personality and needs, but, from the group's point of view, the most valuable behaviors are those that fulfill a need of the group for getting the job done or for sustaining satisfying relationships. If you were to videotape a group, you would notice that one person might take on several different roles during the course of the meeting, or that at different times several people might play the same role. It's not that these roles are assigned, but as a group develops, individuals fill the roles needed to make a group work. Each group is unique in how it fills the roles, and an individual who plays a certain role in one group may play an entirely different role in another setting.

Sometimes individuals unintentionally acquire a "monopoly" on a role. The group will be less effective if capable members are prevented from taking needed roles or from switching roles from time to time. As facilitator, you can serve as a mirror to the group, noting when this is happening and offering suggestions for how to be more fluid with roles. The following chart describes these behaviors.

Group-Oriented Behaviors

TASK-ORIENTED BEHAVIORS

Any behavior that promotes the accomplishment of the task:

- initiates ideas
- seeks or provides information
- summarizes data
- clarifies problems
- questions assumptions
- tests decision making readiness

RELATIONSHIP-ORIENTED BEHAVIORS

Any behavior that promotes group cohesion:

- checks on feeling level of group
- offers encouragement
- promotes inclusion
- resolves conflicts
- is friendly
- gives positive feedback

Self-Oriented Behaviors

Any behavior that diverts the energy of the group, damages group cohesion or group effectiveness:

- arrives late or leaves early
- dampens energy of group
- interprets others' remarks
- holds side conversations
- withholds needed information

- dominates air time
- puts down efforts of others
- "yes, buts" ideas
- ignores group process
- refuses to participate

Overt and Covert Group Issues

A final concept that may be useful in your role of facilitator is the iceberg of group dynamics, developed by W. Brendan Reddy. It is a good reminder that hidden beneath the tip of the iceberg of the group's task are levels of overt and covert group issues, as well as values, beliefs and assumptions and unconscious issues that impact the group. An important rule of thumb is: don't take the group deeper than it needs to go to accomplish its task. And never take a group to a deeper level than you have the time or ability to handle. Facilitation is not therapy.

Great Meetings!

great results

Chapter Three
Getting a Good Start

THE KEY TO GREAT MEETINGS IS PREPARATION. WHETHER IT IS A SHORT MEETING WITH A colleague, a two-day board meeting or a year-long planning process, you will need to allow time for preparing. In the case of the short, informal meeting it may be enough to clarify why you are meeting and what you want out of the time together. In a more complicated meeting, your time will be well spent on the following: assessing the needs of the group; understanding the purpose of the meeting; determining your role and that of others; agreeing who is in charge of which logistical details; deciding how to structure the agenda; and choosing which tools to use.

In this chapter, we will explore the planning and preparation needed in advance of a meeting. Assessment means asking a series of probing questions to be sure you understand what needs to be done to plan a successful meeting. It will mean checking on the purpose of the meeting, the relevant background information, the desired outcomes of the meeting, the people who need to attend, the nature of the group and any internal issues.

Deciding if a Meeting is Necessary

The first step in having a great meeting is to determine if a meeting is, in fact, needed. Nothing makes people happier than being freed from an unnecessary meeting. Follow this flowchart to see if a meeting is necessary.

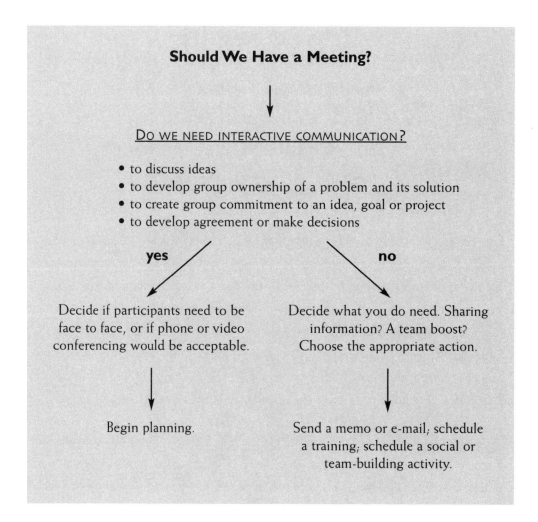

Should We Have a Meeting?

DO WE NEED INTERACTIVE COMMUNICATION?

- to discuss ideas
- to develop group ownership of a problem and its solution
- to create group commitment to an idea, goal or project
- to develop agreement or make decisions

yes / **no**

Decide if participants need to be face to face, or if phone or video conferencing would be acceptable.

Decide what you do need. Sharing information? A team boost? Choose the appropriate action.

Begin planning.

Send a memo or e-mail; schedule a training; schedule a social or team-building activity.

Meetings to Convey Information

Though we have said above that meetings should be held only when interaction is necessary, you may be asked to facilitate a meeting to convey information. Perhaps your leader wants everyone to hear information at the same time, or ensure that everyone receives the same information. If this is the case, think about what aspects of the meeting could be made interactive.

- Would it help if participants heard each other's questions and then the answers to those questions?
- Do you need to ask participants to do some work associated with the information?
- Does the group need to generate a list of next steps, or impacts of the information?

If the answer is no to all of the above, consider other alternatives for sharing information such as email or distribution of written material which provides opportunities to ask questions and requires that people sign off that they have read and understood the material.

If you have decided that a meeting is necessary, be clear about the nature of the information that you need to convey and the role of the participants in working with that information.

If the information is about a policy or directive which has already been decided, and there is not an option for changing or influencing the decision, don't use questions or exercises that ask the participants whether they like the new policy. If it is the participants' job to implement the policy, ask them questions about how they want to carry out the implementation, as long as that is an area over which they can have some control and influence. If the information is about a draft policy or change in procedures, ask participants for their input on the work to date.

Purpose Statements

Once you have determined that a meeting is necessary, your next step is to define the specific purpose for the meeting. Whether you are planning your own meeting, or working on a client's meeting, it is equally important to draft a purpose statement that explains why the group is meeting or why the project is being undertaken. There may be more than one reason. Your group deserves to know what process it is entering and where it is headed.

EXAMPLES OF PURPOSE STATEMENTS:

- The board and staff of the Wildfoot Foundation will clarify all board and staff roles.
- The shipping department staff will develop a work plan for the next quarter.
- The Human Resources Director will meet with all line workers to explain the new benefits package and discuss questions and concerns.
- The second shift packers will discuss recommendations for packing improvements with the management team.
- The board is meeting to develop criteria for fundraising projects.

Remember that the wording of the purpose statement needs to work for all participants. You may have a personal goal of convincing participants to adopt a new fundraising strategy. However, if you word the purpose statement that way, you might make people feel defensive and shut down good interactive communication. Rather than saying "get buy-in to Mario's fundraising strategy" you will want to say something like "choose this year's fundraising strategy by analyzing the pros and cons of two proposals."

Check with yourself or with the person asking you to facilitate. Is the purpose clear? Is it understood and agreed upon by all? Does your own re-examination or your active listening lead you to believe that there is a secondary purpose beyond the presenting one? If so, articulate it. Then restate or reframe the purpose until there is clarity and agreement.

Caution: Keep Your Antennae Up

Sometimes there is a different issue or an underlying problem that needs to be addressed in a forum other than a meeting. Keep your antennae up to make sure the purpose of the meeting makes sense to you and matches what you have heard from others in the organization. Is there a problem with one employee that is being addressed by calling everyone together? Has the purpose of the meeting been identified as discussing new communication strategies when the real issue is trust between management and staff? Even if you aren't sure, trust your instincts when something seems "off."

Desired Outcomes

The desired outcomes define the tangible end products of a meeting. What do you or your client want as a result of the meeting: an agreed-upon decision? A recommendation? A prioritized list of ideas? A list of next steps? Ask yourself: "What does the group want to walk away with at the end of the meeting? Often it takes several variations on these questions to get a clear sense of desired outcomes.

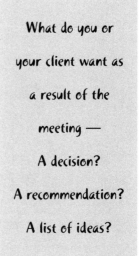

What do you or your client want as a result of the meeting —
A decision?
A recommendation?
A list of ideas?

1. A clear desired outcome statement is a product, not a process. Use nouns in your desired outcomes instead of verbs. Clarity on this point can make all the difference

between a successful and a disappointing meeting.

> A desired
>
> outcome statement
>
> should define a
>
> clear, measurable
>
> goal for the
>
> meeting.

2. A clear desired outcome statement defines a measurable goal for the meeting, such as lists, time lines, a problem statement, etc. Goals such as increased understanding, satisfaction and better attitudes are not measurable and therefore are not very useful desired outcomes.

3. A clear desired outcome statement sets realistic goals for the given time frame of a meeting. You might want to have a detailed strategic plan as an outcome, but that is not realistic in a three-hour meeting. You need to pick a smaller, more manageable outcome. You could establish a number of steps in a longer process and develop desired outcomes for each step along the way, as well as the desired outcome of the total process.

4. A clear desired outcome statement focuses on the format rather than the specific outcome of the meeting. A desired outcome statement should say "final approval of a department budget," rather than "final approval of a $1.5 million department budget."

5. A clear desired outcome statement stays open to the group's process, creativity and needs. If the desired outcome statement says "a list of twelve recommendations," more than twelve ideas may be stifled, and fewer than twelve ideas may feel like failure. The desired outcome should say "a list of recommendations," or use words which provide some wiggle room, such as short, long or a range.

- Short list of ways to improve the communication between our departments, prioritized by cost
- 1-3 recommendations on how to ease the parking problem for first shift
- List of next steps needed in preparing for the December retreat
- Agreed-upon vision statement for our department
- List of ideas regarding responsibilities of a team leader
- Recommendation to the department head for the space needs of the department for the next 24 months (an outcome for the whole process)
  - Definition of the space problems (an outcome for a single meeting)
  - Timeline for accomplishing the work (an outcome for a single meeting)

It is important that the desired outcomes reflect accurately the group's role in the process; the group will come up with the recommendation, a list, a decision. Remember, too, that a desired outcome can change during the meeting. Because of new information or timing, it may no longer be appropriate. For example, part way through a meeting, the group may realize that it isn't ready to develop a time line for a new project (its original desired outcome), but instead needs to define the root problem.

A desired outcome also serves as a way to keep the group on track if it starts to wander off the subject. For example, if the group starts discussing something tangential to the original desired outcome, the facilitator can help the group refocus by restating the desired outcome and asking if the tangent is necessary to reaching that outcome. The time spent understanding and clearly articulating the desired outcomes is a critical part of the preparation for a successful meeting.

Checklist for Meeting Planning

On the following pages are a number of questions to ask yourself or your client as you prepare for a meeting. Answers to these questions will help you design a successful meeting. See also *Chapter Four: Designing a Great Meeting*.

Meeting Preparation Checklist

MEETING PURPOSE, DESIRED OUTCOMES AND TIMEFRAME

- ❑ Is a meeting really needed?

- ❑ What is the purpose of the meeting?

- ❑ What are the desired outcomes of the meeting? What tangible products (lists, decisions, etc.) do you wish to have at the end of the meeting?

- ❑ Is this meeting part of a larger project or series of meetings?

- ❑ Would it be helpful to talk with a wider group of people before planning the meeting? (Different group members may have differing views of the meeting's purpose and desired outcomes.)

- ❑ What is the timeframe within which the work needs to be accomplished?

NATURE OF THE GROUP

- ❑ What is the makeup of the group? Number of people? Position within the organization or community?

- ❑ Are there any special characteristics of the group or its subgroups? (E.g., board members and staff, people for whom English is a second language.)

- ❑ What is the organizational context within which this group works?

- ❑ Who needs to be at the meeting? Remember to include those who have special information, opinions to contribute; those whose approval may be needed in decision-making and those who are expected to carry out the decisions.

Meeting Preparation Checklist, Continued

HISTORY AND CONTEXT

☐ What is the history of the group itself? Has it met before or is it newly formed? What has occurred that might affect how this group works together?

☐ What is the history of the situation leading to the meeting?

☐ Are there any underlying problems or external forces that might impact this meeting?

☐ Has the group had other facilitators? If so, how was that experience?

ROLES

☐ Are there any issues about your real or perceived ability to be a fair facilitator?

☐ Will you be playing dual roles: i.e., facilitator and leader, facilitator and participant, facilitator and expert?

☐ Who will gather and distribute any background information needed for the meeting?

☐ What is the role of the group's leader in this meeting? Participant? Decision maker?

☐ Who will be the recorder?

☐ Who is responsible for typing up and distributing the minutes and group memory?

☐ Who is responsible for the logistics of the meeting? (room reservation, equipment, refreshments, etc.)

☐ What background information will participants need prior to the meeting and who will supply it?

Great Meetings!

great results

Chapter Four
Designing a Great Meeting

Wʜɪʟᴇ ᴇᴀᴄʜ ᴍᴇᴇᴛɪɴɢ ᴅᴇsɪɢɴ ᴡɪʟʟ ʙᴇ ᴅɪꜰꜰᴇʀᴇɴᴛ, ᴛᴀɪʟᴏʀᴇᴅ ᴛᴏ ᴛʜᴇ ɴᴇᴇᴅs ᴏꜰ ᴛʜᴇ sᴘᴇ-cific group, there are certain key elements that are important to consider as you build that unique design.

Each meeting will need three parts: an opening to launch the session and set the stage for the work to be done, the task of the meeting, which may involve one or several steps, as well as a closing so participants leave with a clear understanding of what has been accomplished and what will happen next. Often a group will focus on the task, ignoring the opening and closing. This is akin to trying to eat a sandwich without the bread to hold it together.

These elements may be designed differently for different groups, but you need to include all three elements in each meeting. Often a single meeting is part of a longer, larger project. The whole project design will need to reflect these key elements, as will each individual session.

Opening

The opening, whether very brief or quite extensive, should build a solid foundation from which the group can accompish its task. It should help the participants understand clearly what the task is, why they are doing it, what the hoped for outcome of the meeting is and how they will get there. It should establish how the participants will work with one another and build a conducive environment for doing productive work together. The points below clarify all the items we cover in the opening of a meeting.

1. PURPOSE, OUTCOMES AND AGENDA: The opening should include a review of the purpose and desired outcomes of the meeting. Working from a flipchart, handout or overhead so everyone can see the information at the same time, review these pieces, checking for understanding and agreement. If your preparation has been thorough, there should not be any big surprises or deviations from what you have prepared. But it is possible that a participant may need clarification or may suggest that something be changed. Like the announcement on the airplane, "Welcome to flight number 245 to Cleveland," it is important that everyone in the meeting be headed to the same destination.

   Similarly, it is important to review the agenda so that everyone understands when different subjects will be addressed. Again, you need to check for understanding and agreement. For a longer discussion on developing purpose statements and desired outcomes, see *Chapter Three: Getting a Good Start.*

2. GROUND RULES: Groups determine the parameters of appropriate behavior, procedure and subjects by setting ground rules. The concept of ground rules is

based on the belief that everyone involved in a meeting should be treated equally and fairly. Ground rules explicitly spell out behavior and procedures that people normally consider fair but sometimes abandon in the dynamic interaction of a group. The process of establishing ground rules provides a sanctioned opportunity to discuss what constitutes good behavior and proper procedure. This is particularly helpful as a way to help a contentious group let go of some behavior which has been getting in its way, or to address vague procedures. Some groups may have pre-existing ground rules that can simply be referenced. Others may have such difficulty working together that setting ground rules may take a great deal of time.

The best way to get buy-in is to have the group define its own ground rules for the meeting. If you feel that the group has overlooked an area that should be addressed, such as confidentiality, ask them to consider it and decide how they would like to handle it. As facilitator, you can ask for ground rules that you know you will need for yourself. Be sure to check for agreement, asking if everyone is willing to live by the ground rules. During the meeting, the group can enforce its own rules and you can refer to them as necessary. Ground rules can also be added along the way as needed.

It is best to write out the ground rules, especially for a group that will be meeting on an on-going basis. Then, at the beginning of each meeting, the list of ground rules can be unfurled and available for everyone to review. The time spent establishing ground rules usually pays off handsomely by both keeping the group on track and maintaining good relations.

As a facilitator, ground rules are valuable because they transfer much of the responsibility for enforcement of correct behavior, procedure and structure to the group. You can stand by the flipchart and point to the ground rule, reminding the group of its agreement, rather than confront the behavior in the group.

In their book, <u>Managing Public Disputes</u> (Jossey-Bass, San Francisco, 1988) Susan L. Carpenter and W.J.D. Kennedy describe three types of ground rules: behavioral, procedural and substantive. Briefly, behavioral ground rules describe the ways people treat and interact with one another. Procedural ground rules include any guidelines for the process or mechanics of the meeting. Substantive ground rules describe the content boundaries that govern discussion during a meeting. Each group has its own needs regarding the use and wording of ground rules.

Sample Ground Rules to Consider

BEHAVIORAL:

- One person talks at a time
- No side conversations
- Use language that does not stereotype others
- We value different opinions; debate ideas, not people
- Take responsibility to speak up if you have something to say
- What is said here stays here

PROCEDURAL:

- When one of us leaves the room, the discussion stops (or will continue)
- Meetings will begin on time and end on time
- Turn off cell phones
- During conference calls, call on each person in order
- Decision making will be by levels of consensus, with voting as a fall back
- Substitutes are (or are not) acceptable

SUBSTANTIVE:

- We will only discuss issues over which we have direct control
- We will discuss the office as a whole, but not individual departments
- We will talk only about the future, not the past

Hints for Establishing Ground Rules

Groups are sometimes resistant to establishing ground rules. Their reluctance may come from the time it takes, because they feel it is childish to define good behavior, or because they may have created ground rules before that were ignored.

A declaration that you, as facilitator, need the ground rules, and a promise to keep the process of generating ground rules "crisp," as well as a sense of humor, is usually enough to engage the group.

In some situations, you may decide to bring a list of suggested ground rules, rather than generate them all in the group. Large groups, public meetings, groups unfamiliar with ground rules and even groups that might be hostile to the idea of taking time to generate ground rules, can benefit from your "priming the pump" with ground rules. Remember to check for buy-in for the ground rules you bring, and don't hesitate to cross out any that create discomfort in the group.

IN GENERATING GROUND RULES WE USE THIS PROCESS:

1. Ask for suggestions for ground rules. All ideas are welcome.

    Example: A group member says, "I want everyone to be polite."

2. Define the suggestion in terms of behavior. Asking "what would it look like if..." helps.

    Example: The facilitator says, "John, what would it look like to you if everyone were being polite?"

    John: "No one would interrupt anyone and there would be no personal attacks."

    Facilitator: "So you are proposing two ground rules; no interruptions and no personal attacks? "

3. Check with yourself to see if the ground rules really serve the group. If not, explain your concern to the group and offer an alternative

4. Check for consensus on the ground rule.

5. Write it up on the flipchart.

6. After the ground rules are written, confirm that everyone can abide by them. Ask your group, "Is there anything that you don't understand? Anything you need to change or add, in order to be able to live with these?"

3. ROLES: It is important to clarify all roles in the group: facilitator, leader, expert, participant. Is the leader present to listen, offer expert information, make decisions? Is your role to focus exclusively on facilitation or will you be a participant as well? For a discussion on dual roles, see *Chapter Two: Getting a Good Start*. Participants need to be clear about their expected role, as well. Following are sample role definitions.

Sample Role Definitions

FACILITATOR: "I am your facilitator for this meeting. I have helped to design the agenda and will be leading you through the process. I will not contribute any ideas on the content of the meeting. It is my job to make it easier for you to arrive at your own agreements." Or, "I've agreed to facilitate today, but I also will participate from time to time and will let you know when I change roles."

LEADER: "I have called this meeting today for us to decide on a solution for the parking problems. I have asked Mary to facilitate and would like someone to volunteer to record. (Or, I will be facilitating myself and contributing my ideas from time to time.) I will be participating with the group. I would like this group to arrive at consensus on how to solve this problem. If that is not possible, I will make the decision personally, based on the ideas raised in the group."

RECORDER: "I will be recording and will try to capture your ideas on the board. If I miss anything or haven't gotten it quite right, please let me know so that I can correct it. I will (or will not) ask for time to participate and add my own ideas."

PARTICIPANTS: "Our role as participants is to contribute, generate the content, listen carefully, share concerns and ideas candidly, act constructively, and make commitments."

4. DECISION MAKING METHODS: There are many ways that groups can make decisions and it is important that the group be clear in advance which method or combination of methods it wants to use. Some decision making techniques are:

- Majority voting
- Voting with two-thirds, three-quarters or higher percentage required
- Deferring to a subgroup
- Consensus with a back up
- Consensus without a back up

> If the group believes it is empowered to make a final decision and finds out later it was only a recommendation, the members will feel deceived.

It is also important to be clear about the group's role in the decision making process. Are they being asked to give recommendations, or to make a decision themselves? If the group believes that it is empowered to make a final decision and finds out later that it was only a recommendation, the members will feel deceived. Refer to *Chapter Five: Understanding Process* for a more detailed description of decision making.

5. PARKING LOT: This useful tool (which has many names — basket, bin, parking lot) provides a place for ideas that are off the subject of the agenda. The ideas may belong later in the agenda, may be relevant to a future meeting's agenda or might simply be off topic. Title a flipchart page "Parking Lot" (or whatever name you are using) and post it throughout the meeting. This process allows the group to acknowledge and save ideas without getting sidetracked by them. It also helps reduce the repetition of the "one track mind" participant by having her issue up on the chart with a promise to deal with it eventually.  The group must return to the parking lot by the end of the meeting to decide when and how those issues will be handled. It should not be used as a trash can!

6. NEXT STEPS CHART: You may want to post a prepared next steps chart (what, who, when) at the meeting opening. Record on the chart any steps the group identifies that need to be taken.

7. GROUP FORMING: There are several aspects of group forming, ranging from the simplest of gestures that set a constructive tone to significant efforts at team building. Using the information gathered during your early preparation, you need to decide what kind of group forming would be useful for your meeting. Remember that doing work in groups is hard and demands some level of trust and ability to work together. Consider the following three levels of group building to see what is needed for your agenda. Then, refer to *Chapter Seven: Maximizing Your Group's Potential*, for details on group building techniques.

> Setting the Tone: The facilitator sets the tone for the meeting from the moment participants walk through the door. By greeting people cheerfully and introducing yourself, welcoming them, indicating that you are glad they came, and thanking them for their participation, you are setting a positive, constructive tone from the start. If you are a member of the group, make sure you greet everyone, not just those whom you know well or with whom you share similar views.

> Introductions: The nature of the group, how long it has been working together, and the nature of the issue it is working on will determine what kind of introductions and warm-up exercises are most appropriate.

> Team Building: If the group needs to build a higher level of trust or establish more common ground, you may choose to plan some team building or trust building work into the opening of the meeting before the group gets to the more difficult work or decision making.

Task

The central part of the meeting is the task that needs to be accomplished by the group. There may be more than one task, depending on the desired outcomes for the meeting. To build the agenda for this part of the meeting, work directly from your desired outcomes and decide for each one what process steps need to be taken to arrive at the desired outcome.

For example, if the desired outcome is a list of roles and duties for the new executive director, look at what the group needs to do to complete a list that will serve them well. Do they need information about the roles of the previous director, or about another position they are using for bench marking? Do they need information on typical executive directors in order to get started? Or do they need to break loose from old formats and think outside the box? Each of those circumstances would require a different process approach. Is the group large or small? The size could determine which technique you use for generating ideas.

In *Chapter Five: Understanding Process*, we outline the process steps that a group must take as it defines and analyzes a problem, envisions the desired goal and comes to agreement on solutions. These steps along with the tools and techniques detailed in chapters six and seven will help you design this task section.

As you are designing your agenda and picking the tools, be sure you choose a tool that will lead you to your desired outcome. If you want a prioritized list of options, pick a tool that gives you a list in priority order. See "Hints for Choosing the Right Tool" on page 79 of *Chapter Six: Choosing the Right Tool*.

Also be sure you are asking the group the right questions. For example, if the boss has already made the decision to change a policy, don't ask the group what it thinks of the change. Ask the group how best to implement it or what they need to be able to implement it.

Closing

Just as a meeting needs clarity in the beginning, it needs clarity at the end. Participants need to leave the meeting with a clear, common understanding of what has been accomplished, what decisions have been made, what needs to happen next and who is assigned to do what by when. In addition, it is valuable to evaluate the meeting, so that the next meeting can be improved and the group can congratulate itself on what went well. Lastly, at the conclusion of some meetings or projects personal closure is necessary.

1. REVIEW GROUP AGREEMENTS AND DECISIONS: Reiterate or even make a separate list of the decisions the group has agreed upon in the course of the meeting. For example:

   Decisions: Frieda will continue as substitute receptionist until March 1.
   Anna and Bill will share Frieda's work until March 1.
   The department picnic will be held March 5.

2. IDENTIFY NEXT STEPS: In order to ensure follow through, it is important that there are clear assignments to which everyone agrees. The following chart helps to make the follow through clear.

What	Who	Date
1. Type and circulate minutes	Josh	4/25
2. Review decisions with VP	Anita	4/29

3. CHECK THE PARKING LOT: While this is not the time to deal with the content of each parking lot item, it is important to do a quick check to determine whether the parking lot items are still relevant and, if so, when and by whom they will be addressed. If there is disagreement about an item's relevance, move to deciding when to continue that discussion. This process reinforces that the parking lot is a valuable meeting tool, not a trash can.

4. EVALUATE THE MEETING: At the very end of the meeting it is useful to take five minutes to evaluate what went well and what should be changed or improved upon next time. The suggestions can run from needing a break or refreshments, to comments on the space, to the need for more participation. This provides valuable information to help improve each subsequent meeting. A simple chart showing the positives and what to change will do.

+ What Worked	Δ Changes or Upgrades
• stuck to agenda • excellent facilitation • everyone participated	• too many tasks for time timeframe • needed bigger room

5. CONSIDER PERSONAL CLOSURE: When a group has completed a long or challenging piece of work or is disbanding, participants will have formed a special bond or learned to work with each other in a new way. The participants may need a way to have personal closure, acknowledging and thanking one another or saying good bye.

Meeting Location and Facilities

The details of where the meeting is held or how the room is equipped may seem minor, but they can have an impact on the success of your meeting. A room which is the wrong size, uncomfortable or ill-equipped will make it harder for the group to be productive.

LOCATION:

- Convenient: Meetings take enough time without adding unnecessary travel time.
- Quiet and separate from work: Meetings are more productive if they are away from the interruptions of traffic, phone calls, other people stopping in with messages and questions, etc.
- Neutral: Meetings that are part of resolving disputes may need to be held on neutral territory so that neither party or group feels at a disadvantage.

FACILITIES: Some factors to consider:

- right size
- appropriate break out space for small groups, if necessary
- accessible for people with disabilities
- comfortable lighting
- appropriate collection of chairs and tables (preferably movable ones)
- plenty of wall space for hanging flipchart paper
- necessary equipment: flipcharts, tape, markers, black board, overhead projector, handouts, etc.

Hints for Taking Charge of the Meeting Space

Ideally, a meeting space allows for flexible arrangements with plenty of elbow room. Whether you have been able to choose a space to fit your needs, or are using the only space available, take charge of the space to maximize its effectiveness for the group:

- Arrange for wall space to hang flipcharts and other graphics. Take down movable objects. Get permission to tape over pictures, posters, etc. (If you use draft tape you minimize the potential for damage to such items.)

- Orient the chairs and tables to the wall space if appropriate.

- Create a sense of group. Eliminate extra chairs. If possible, arrange the seating so everyone can see each other easily.

- If there are windows, arrange the room so glare is minimized.

SEATING ARRANGEMENTS: Being seated at a table is comfortable for most people. It helps define their personal space, not to mention giving them somewhere to put their notes and coffee. If you choose to remove tables, have a clear purpose in doing so.

- For groups of 2-8 people, a small round table is good to create a sense of informality and collaboration.
- For medium sized groups (8-30 people), tables set up in a "U" shape allow everyone to see each other. This shape also provides the facilitator access to the group through the center of the U. If the tables used are small, you can increase visibility by creating an octagon with one open end.

- Large groups (30-200 people) do well at a series of round tables. This arrangement gives people connection to a smaller group and is a good set up for small group exercises or discussions. If you want everyone to face forward, provide seats around the table, but leave the side facing the front vacant.

Seating Arrangement Examples

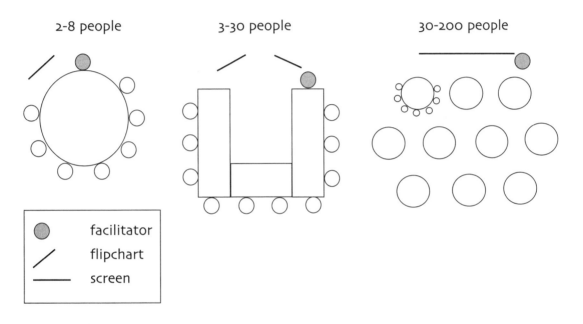

2-8 people   3-30 people   30-200 people

facilitator	
flipchart	
screen	

Agenda Planning

The facilitator's working agenda will be highly detailed, providing all the notes you will need for yourself. The agenda for the group will be less detailed, providing the what, when and who. The group doesn't need to know what methods you are planning to use to accomplish the agenda; besides, you may well change those methods depending on the progress of the group. The agenda should be sent out in advance, posted for the meeting and reviewed at the opening of the meeting with the group. On the following page is an example of an agenda planning sheet.

Agenda Planning Worksheet

DATE OF MEETING: TIME: LOCATION:

MEETING PURPOSE:

TIMEFRAME	TOPIC	METHOD	WHO
Opening	Introductions, Review: purpose, outcomes, agenda, roles, rules		
Task			
Closing	Review decisions, Acknowledge accomplishments, Identify next steps, Check parking lot, Evaluate meeting		

Great Meetings!

great results

Chapter Five
Understanding Process

THERE ARE MANY DIFFERENT KINDS OF MEETINGS — MEETINGS TO generate a vision, to reconcile disputing parties, to develop a plan, to solve a problem and so on. In most meetings there are steps that you move through to provide the input for ultimately making a decision. It is a process of making change. That change may be from a good situation to a better one, from a bad situation to an acceptable one, from a current situation to a different future, or something else in between. Whether you are doing long-range planning or solving a problem, you need to know the process steps that will help you bring the work to a successful conclusion.

> As facilitator, you need to know the process steps that will help you bring the work to a successful conclusion.

Generally speaking, there are three process steps to consider:

1. ISSUE: Analysis of the problem, the current situation or the context of the group's work.

2. GOAL: Envisioning the ideal, an image of the desired future state, the goal or a target.

3. DECISION: Decision making, which includes generating and evaluating options.

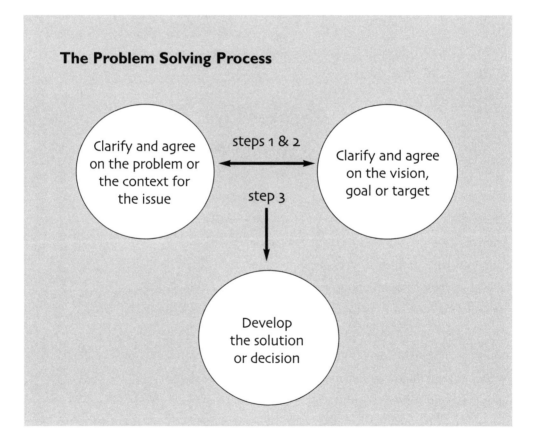

The Problem Solving Process

Clarify and agree on the problem or the context for the issue

steps 1 & 2

Clarify and agree on the vision, goal or target

step 3

Develop the solution or decision

The sequence of these steps is not necessarily linear. Depending on the desired outcome of the meeting or the context of the meeting, the group may choose to start at different places in the process. For instance, if you have a group that is feeling discouraged, you may begin a process by visioning the ideal, which will give them more energy and engagement, and later return to the current context or problem. Or, if the meeting task is to solve a specific, immediate issue, it may be more helpful to start with an agreement on and analysis of the problem.

There is, however, one critical tenet of process steps. Whether you are doing long range planning or solving a problem, you can't just leap into solutions or next steps (Step #3). You need to lay the ground work by building a common understanding of the background, context or problem and by agreeing on what you are trying to accomplish or where you are going. In order to generate a viable solution, you first need agreement on the nature of the problem.

Process Steps

Below you will find comments on each of the three process steps and tools that can be used effectively in that stage. Each tool is described in detail in *Chapter Six: Choosing the Right Tool*, and is organized by category. This is not an exhaustive list. Use whatever tools work for you and your group.

1. DEFINING AND ANALYZING THE CONTEXT, ISSUE OR PROBLEM

    An often overlooked process step is developing a clear definition of the presenting issue or reason for coming together. Participants in a group may have very different ideas about what the issue or problem really is. The effectiveness of the rest of the process depends on clear, common understanding of this background. As much as possible, build a shared definition of the problem, rather than defining it strictly as one person's or one side's problem.

    When it comes to defining the problem, insist that people provide specific

When defining

a problem,

insist that people

provide specific

descriptions

or examples.

descriptions or examples. If someone says, "The problem is the way this town is run," ask for specific ways in which he sees a problem with town management. Language that is vague or carries value judgments is impossible to work with in the problem solving process. Terms such as good or bad, efficient or inefficient are all subjective terms that need concrete definition.

If the stated problems appear to be more of a cause than the real problem, push for deeper levels by asking why it's a problem. For example: Quentin says, "The problem is flextime." As facilitator, you ask, "Why is that a problem?" Quentin answers, "Because there are not enough people here at 8:00 to answer the phones." "Why is that a problem?" "It means we aren't serving our customers." "Why is that a problem?" "It means we are potentially damaging the viability of our business." The challenge in this process is to know when you have reached an appropriate level of problem. If you continue to ask why is that a problem, you may find yourself in larger realms than you are able to affect.

Another way to look at problem definition, when there is not an obvious presenting problem, is to do a definition of the current situation asking questions such as:

- What do you like about the current situation and want to save?
- What would you like to change?
- What are the strengths and weaknesses of the current organization?
- What external threats are there to the organization?
- What opportunities are out there?

In this step, you may want to gather information and data in advance of the meeting to help the group move along in the process. You may be able to use email to survey people in the group for their opinions or background information. It can be shared with everyone simultaneously or, if anonymity is important, all responses can come to you and be collated into a single report, which analyzes the themes but does not show individual's responses. The group may need to collect outside information from others in the organization, from stakeholder groups, from technical experts, or through background research before clearly identifying the problem, or before generating ideas or evaluating options. The group should agree what information is needed, how it will be gathered and who is responsible. The needed information could be a simple set of figures or an elaborate series of focus groups, surveys and public meetings. In contentious situations, agreeing on the source of the information can be a significant first step. Having neutral, mutually acceptable data is important in a dispute.

Tools for Defining and Analyzing the Problem

- Brainstorming, pg 80
- Brain Mapping, pg 92
- Fish Bone Diagram,
  pg 94

- Picture It, pg 96
- SWOT Analysis, pg 98
- What Is/Isn't the
  Problem, pg 100

2. VISIONING THE IDEAL GOAL, TARGET OR PREFERRED FUTURE STATE

Visioning is the process of identifying the ideal state of a situation. In its early stages, the vision may be a broad view of the ideal state. For example, if a group is focused on improving the local high school, the vision may describe "students excited about learning, well-paid teachers, state-of-the-art facilities and no drop outs."

However, in order to turn the vision into an attainable goal, the group needs to develop a clear statement of the desired result. By the time a vision is translated into a goal, it should be put in a time context and be described in measurable terms so that the group can tell whether it has actually achieved the goal. It should also be positive and inspiring, something which the group is excited about accomplishing.

There may also be multiple goals, but generally no more than six or seven. The ideal goal should make statements about the future, not action steps about how to get there. For example, "By the end of the 4 year plan, the drop out rate from Morris High School will be below 7%, teachers' salaries will be at least 5% above the state average and a new multipurpose building will be built."

If a group is discouraged or divided, it can be useful to begin with the vision step as a motivator and a way to find common ground before working on a problem definition.

> If a group is
> discouraged
> or divided, try
> visioning as
> a motivator.

Tools for Visioning the Ideal

- Wish, Want, Wonder, pg 101
- Newspaper Article About the Future, pg 102
- Picture the Path to the Future, pg 104
- Defining the Vision, pg 105

3. GENERATING A SOLUTION OR DECISION

Now that you understand the current issue and you know where you are headed, it is time to identify a solution or decision based on the desired outcome(s) you developed for the meeting. You want to be able to activate the creativity of the group, look at lots of possibilities and, in the end, help the group come to a conclusion. There are three sub-steps under Generating a Solution or Decision, that are useful in fact in any of the process steps. In each step, you may want to generate ideas, evaluate options and decide on the preferred options. The sub-steps are as follows:

A. GENERATE - Generating ideas: This is an expansive phase of the process and you want to encourage groups to consider all possible options. To have a successful idea generating session, you need to guide the group away from two situations: any attempt to critique ideas or to settle prematurely on one option. The idea is to generate as many creative ideas as possible. Encourage people to look beyond the obvious, to be silly or outrageous — but above all to be creative. To do this requires a safe place where the participants know they won't be rejected for any idea. Do not permit any evaluation during brainstorming or react yourself in a negative or dismissive way to any ideas. It's equally important not to react in an enthusiastic way to one idea or another. Use your enthusiasm to praise the process. For example, "You are coming up with a great list. There are lots of creative ideas here!"

> Do not permit any evaluation during brainstorming, or react yourself in any way. Use your enthusiasm to praise the process.

Tools for Generating Ideas

- Brainstorming (and variations), pg 80

- Brain Mapping, pg 92

> If you are unclear, there's a good chance that someone in the group is also unclear, so ask and encourage questions.

B.   EVALUATE - Clarifying, evaluating and narrowing ideas: After options have been generated, the next step is to check for understanding of the ideas. Make sure everyone is clear about what is meant by each statement on the list; the narrowing process will be faulty if group members have a different understanding of what statements mean. Remember: if you are unclear, there is a good chance that someone in the group is also unclear, so ask and encourage questions at this stage.

For many facilitators, the next steps of evaluating and narrowing are the most challenging. In brainstorming, you were careful to steer the group away from evaluative comments. Now it is time for the group to look at the list critically. Invite the group to comment on the ideas they have generated. Ask for any observations or concerns they may have about the ideas generated. Listen carefully and be ready to follow up on concerns expressed.

Once the group has concluded its comments and concerns have been resolved (often easier said than done!) you must now select the right tool for evaluating and narrowing options. It is important that you and the group are clear about what kind of evaluating and narrowing is needed.

The following questions will help you choose which decision making tools to use:

- Do you need to prioritize the list?
- Do you need to compare options to a set of criteria?
- Do you need to decide yes or no to an idea?
- Do you want to combine compatible ideas or eliminate unworkable ones?

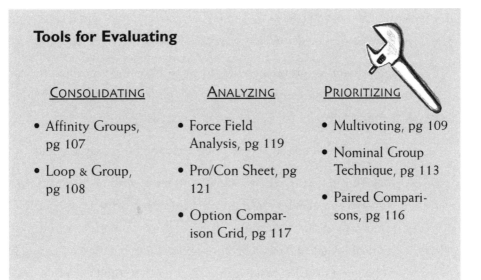

Tools for Evaluating

CONSOLIDATING	ANALYZING	PRIORITIZING
• Affinity Groups, pg 107	• Force Field Analysis, pg 119	• Multivoting, pg 109
• Loop & Group, pg 108	• Pro/Con Sheet, pg 121	• Nominal Group Technique, pg 113
	• Option Comparison Grid, pg 117	• Paired Comparisons, pg 116

C. DECIDE - Making the final decision: Now it's time to make a final decision. At this stage, the facilitator can help the group by summarizing the results of the evaluating and narrowing process and reminding the group of the desired outcome for the meeting. For example, "You have sorted through a number of options for software packages to purchase for the department. After comparing the six choices, the Zoom package best meets the criteria. Our desired outcome for today is a recommendation for our preferred software package." Before you finish, do one last check for clarity, "Are you ready to make a final decision? Is there any further discussion you want to have before we check for agreement?"

At the beginning of the meeting, the group will have agreed which decision making method to use. Following is a more in depth discussion about decision making methods.

Consensus: Increasingly, many work groups choose consensus as their decision making method. The advantage is that when a group reaches consensus, everyone "buys in" to the decision. The major disadvantage is that consensus can take a great deal of time. For a streamlined approach to consensus, see "Levels of Consensus" in *Chapter Six: Choosing the Right Tool.*

It is important for group members to share a common meaning for consensus and to have agreement about what to do if they do not reach consensus. If the group decides to use consensus, it needs to:

1. discuss and adopt an agreed-upon meaning for consensus; and

2. decide whether it will use "pure" consensus, with no alternative method for decision making, or "modified" consensus, with a fall-back method (such as voting or executive decision) in place. Both can work; what is critical is that the group be clear about which method it is using before it begins a decision making process. It is also useful to define precisely the circumstances under which the fall-back method will be used (the time limit is reached, for minor decisions, etc.). Where a hierarchical fall-back process is in place, it is important for the person in charge to convey clearly when the group has control of the decision making and at what point she will have the final word.

> Sense of the group honors the group as an entity that is more than the sum of its individual members.

<u>Sense of the Group</u>: The facilitator, leader or a group member may choose to state the sense of the group. This is a summary of what that person understands and feels the decision of the group to be. Sense of the group honors the group as an entity that is more than the sum of its individual members. Thus there may not be unanimity of agreement coming from every individual, yet the decision is clear for the group. Any time someone speaks her sense of the group, it must be checked out and agreed upon by the group.

Voting: Voting is a commonly used decision making method. The advantages of voting are that it is quick and gives a decisive result. A disadvantage is that the results leave winners and losers, and losers may not support the decision with as much enthusiasm as winners. When a group chooses voting as its decision making method, it should be clear which of the following it is choosing to use:

Simple Majority: The decision is made by choosing a solution which is acceptable to more than half the entire group, with each person having equal power (one person, one vote).

Super Majority: The decision is made by choosing a solution which is acceptable to more than 2/3 or 3/4 of the entire group, with each person having equal power (one person, one vote).

Majority - Minority Opinion - Majority: The decision is made by holding a straw vote. If the result is less than unanimous, the "minority" are asked to explain why they are voting against the issue. Then a final binding vote is held.

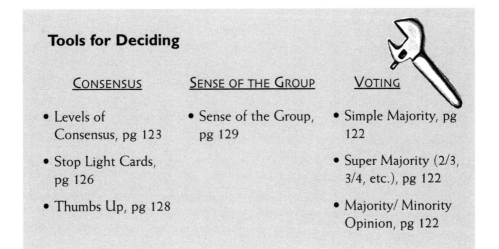

Tools for Deciding

CONSENSUS	SENSE OF THE GROUP	VOTING
• Levels of Consensus, pg 123	• Sense of the Group, pg 129	• Simple Majority, pg 122
• Stop Light Cards, pg 126		• Super Majority (2/3, 3/4, etc.), pg 122
• Thumbs Up, pg 128		• Majority/ Minority Opinion, pg 122

Long Range/Strategic Planning

We are frequently asked about which specialized tools are needed for strategic or long range planning. Our approach to this type of planning involves elements of both content and process.

Long range and strategic planning are two comparable phrases for describing a process often used by groups to develop goals and a plan for the future. It is essential for an organization to know and agree on where it is going and how it wants to get there. Good planning involves having adequate background data, understanding the current situation and external context, defining the desired vision, identifying goals and setting the steps to get to those goals. Sometimes the process involves re-examining the organization's mission as well.

Many people have their own definitions of the words that are commonly used in long range/strategic planning. The following is a glossary of how we are using and defining some of these common terms in this book.

LONG RANGE: Long range is more than one year. In most businesses or organizations a long range plan looks out three to five years. If the organization is in a period of rapid transition one to two years may be as far out as it can reasonably project. On the other hand, a group talking about large capital investments may need a five to ten year vision with a shorter time frame for the detailed business plan.

STRATEGIC: A strategic plan or process is one which maps out the necessary strategies, steps or action plans to get from the current situation an ideal one. It means planning and taking steps which are calculated to achieve a long range goal in a methodical manner.

VISION: A vision is a full picture or rich description of what the organization looks like, the way the participants want it to be, at some point in the future. It contains details on what people are doing, saying, or feeling. It describes the clients or customers, the physical facilities, the budget and sources of revenue, the products, technology, competition and whatever else is important to identify.

GOALS: The goals are the specific, large scale accomplishments the group or organization wants to achieve by a future date. Think of them as targets to aim for. Goals should be specific, clear and stated as a completed accomplishment. They should also be measurable. The list of goals is usually short (from three to six items) and is drawn directly from the vision.

OBJECTIVES, ACTION STEPS, BUSINESS PLAN AND STRATEGIES: These are all terms for the steps moving from the current situation to the goals. Objectives are the sub-goals that need to be accomplished on the way to a major goal. Action steps are specific things to do to achieve a larger goal. A business plan outlines how to move forward, quarter by quarter, identifying the step, the implications for the budget and/or staffing, the person in charge and the time frame. Strategies are the plans you make as you figure out "how to" get to the desired future.

> Objectives are the sub-goals that need to be accomplished on the way to a major goal.

Key Components of the Long Range Planning Process

- a definition of the current state and context of the organization
- a vision of the future
- key goals
- a plan for how to get there

As indicated in the Planning Process graphic below, you need to have a good understanding of where you are, be clear about where you want to end up (vision) and what you want to accomplish (goals), and then develop a plan for how to get there (how to), just like the process steps outlined earlier in the chapter.

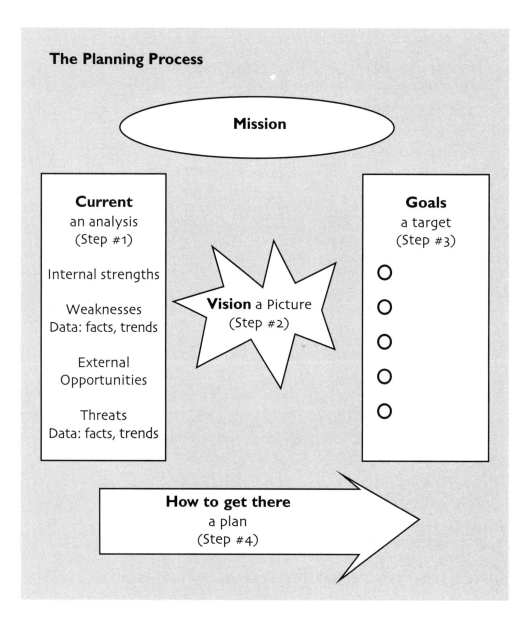

The Planning Process

Mission

Current
an analysis
(Step #1)

Internal strengths

Weaknesses
Data: facts, trends

External
Opportunities

Threats
Data: facts, trends

Vision a Picture
(Step #2)

Goals
a target
(Step #3)

How to get there
a plan
(Step #4)

Process Steps in Long Range Planning

UNDERSTANDING THE CURRENT SITUATION: A group needs good information on which to base its planning. Participants need to understand the current issues of the organization as well as the broader context within which the organization works. Depending on the complexity of the organization and the depth of its planning process, this work can be developed briefly with a SWOT analysis (see page 98 of *Chapter Six: Choosing the Right Tool*) to collect the group's ideas on the strengths and weaknesses of the organization itself and the opportunities and threats that face the group from outside. Or, it could be an extended effort to collect input from clients, customers, staff and various stakeholders through meetings, surveys or interviews. The extent of information collected depends on the group's need for enough information to make informed projections and decisions about the organization's future. Decisions based on anecdotes or poor background information could send the group off in an unproductive or unrealistic direction.

> Decisions based on anecdotes or poor information could send the group off in an unproductive direction.

Background information can include:

- SWOT analysis
- Surveys, interviews and meetings with stakeholders
- Data on relevant trends, both internal and external to the organization
- Relevant articles

DEVELOPING THE DESIRED VISION: Armed with a solid base of information, the group is ready to imagine the future of the organization. How far out should the group be looking for its vision? It depends on the circumstances within which the group is working. A group in a very volatile situation where events are changing rapidly will be hard pressed to get a good read on anything that is further out than two years. An organization that is stable and operating in an environment that is not changing dramatically can easily look out five years. Groups looking to make large capital investments, such as, new buildings or moving to a new location, may need to look out as far as ten years for that part of the vision. But they will need to have intermediate plans that are shorter for the operating part of the organization.

To do the visioning, develop a visioning exercise that is tailored to the needs of the group. See the section on visioning beginning on page 101 of *Chapter Six: Choosing the Right Tool*. For example, if a manufacturing unit is looking at significant changes in technologies over the next several years, be sure to prompt them to envision how the product is being made. If a non-profit is looking at significant changes in the demographics in its area, prompt them to envision the client base that they will be serving and the services they will provide. How wild and crazy should their description of the ideal be? Ask them to stretch and reach for what they want, even if it might be difficult to achieve. But at the same time, their visioning needs to be grounded in the reality of the data they have collected. Ask them to imagine a full, rich video of the future complete with sound track. When you have collected a summary of their work, you will have a list of the key elements that the group agrees should be part of their vision of the future.

> Ask them to stretch and reach for what they want, even if it might be difficult to achieve.

DEVELOPING GOALS: Once the key elements of the vision are clear, the goals should flow naturally from that work. The vision was a full color video with sound track. The goals name succinctly the key accomplishments of the organization by the end of the time period. Goals are the targets to aim for. They must be specific enough so that the group will know whether they have been accomplished. They are larger than the detailed steps for how to get there. It is hard for an organization to stay focused on a long list of goals; a short list (two to six) is usually best.

Sample goals:

- In (name the year) XYZ's process for making widgets will be fully automated and producing at least 200 widgets an hour. *Not: In (name the year) XYZ will be better at producing widgets faster.*
- In (name the year) the I Can Fly Program will be serving youth from all district middle and high schools with year round programs in multiple locations. *Not: The I Can Fly Program will serve more kids than currently.*

BUILDING A PLAN FOR HOW TO GET THERE: Now comes the more detailed work of figuring out how to get from the present to the desired future and goals. In a small, Board driven organization or in a company work team, this step may be done directly by the people who developed the vision and goals. In a larger organization, staff or sub-committees may develop a plan for approval by the Board or appropriate executive. Basically, the group is working to answer the question of how to get from today to the desired future. That work may include an examination of the obstacles they need to overcome and the forces that will help them to move forward (see the section on Force Field Analysis on page 119 of *Chapter Six: Choosing the Right Tool*). It may include more brainstorming sessions on the intervening steps needed for each of the goals and more data gathering. It should certainly include a time line indicating the group's expectation of when different steps should be accomplished as well as assignments for who is responsible to get them done. It should indicate the budgetary implications of the different steps. It may establish mechanisms for evaluating success or impact. When completed, the plan should be a clear blueprint for how the organization is going to manage its finances, manpower and other resources to accomplish its goals, and what the intermediate objectives are along the way.

Plan for How to Get There

Goal #1: By the year 2007 the I Can Fly Program will be serving youth from both middle and high schools county wide with year round programs in multiple locations.

TASK	BUDGET/STAFF IMPLICATION	WHO	WHEN
YEAR ONE			
Identify funding sources for expanded programs	time from existing staff	James	by 3/15
Set up joint committee with school to develop program ideas and identify at risk students	time from existing staff	Elaine	by 2/15
Manage ongoing committee work	time from existing staff student intern - no cost	Elaine	through 12/30
YEAR TWO			
Committee work is written up into a case statement	time from existing staff	Joshua	by 1/30
Write grant applications for funding	$1,200, hire grants writer some staff time	James	by 3/21

Questions to Answer Before You Start a Planning Process

- What kind of a product do you want from your planning process?
- Who needs to be included in the process and how?
- What is the timeframe for the planning process?
- Are you running it in house or looking for a professional facilitator to help guide the process?
- What kind of background information do you need to make informed decisions about the future?

Specialized Approaches to Process

There are some specialized meeting structures. The following are some of the better known and more widely used. We will give a brief description of the meeting structure, when it might be useful and how to find more complete information.

OPEN SPACE: Open Space Technology was developed by Harrison Owen in 1984 to capture in a meeting format the level of interest and engagement that people exhibited when they talked informally about subjects that were important to them. The meeting structure allows people to select and work on what is important to them within the context of a subject area. Participants are invited to a meeting on a general subject with no detailed agenda. At the meeting, they are invited to suggest a sub-topic of the general subject, which interests them enough to lead a group of people in discussing and looking for common ground in that sub-topic. Participants are then invited to sign up for the sub-topics that interest them, leading to a self-selected group of interested participants. At the end of the allotted time, each group is responsible for writing up and sharing with others the results of their group's work, using computers and copying equipment. Every participant ends up with the results from every group. The technique can be used with large or small groups and is particularly useful for complex questions where the differing points of view create the possibility of conflict.

For more information on Open Space Technology consult the following books by Harrison Owen: <u>Open Space Technology: A User's Guide, second edition,</u> 1997 (Berrett-Koehler Publishers, Inc, San Francisco); <u>Expanding Our Now: The Story of Open Space Technology</u>; <u>Tales from Open Space</u>. You can check the web site of **www.openspaceworld.org** as well.

FUTURE SEARCH CONFERENCES: Future Search Conferences have a long history going back to Gestalt psychologists and objective relations analysts in the early part of the 20th Century. Currently, Marvin R. Weisbord has become the leader of this process in the United States. It is a structured, participatory planning process designed to enable the participants to direct their own future based on an understanding of their past and present, a confirmation of common values and a commitment to action. It relies on bringing together a broad cross section of "stakeholders" to explore common ground. The four basic principles are:

- "Whole system" in the room
- Global context as backdrop for local action
- Future focus and common ground rather than conflict and problems
- Self management and personal responsibility

Future Search Conferences can be done in small groups and single organizations dealing with an internal issue or in whole communities facing broad social issues.

For more information consult <u>Discovering Common Ground</u> by Marvin R. Weisbord and 35 International Coauthors (Berrett-Koehler Publishers, San Fancisco, 1992) or **www.futuresearch.net**.

APPRECIATIVE INQUIRY: Appreciative Inquiry has its roots in the work of David Cooperrider and Suresh Srivastva. It is based on the principle that a company, organization or community can unleash its creativity and energy for positive change by focusing on the positive and envisioning the common, desired future. It asks what is the best the whole system has to offer (achievements, assets, unexplored potential and so on) and what the system looks like when it is the way the group wants it to be. Working from this appreciative approach the group describes its desired future and sets goals for itself. For more information consult A Positive Revolution in Change: Appreciative Inquiry by David Cooperrider and Diana Whitney, Appreciative Inquiry Handbook, by David L. Copperrider, it al, The Thin Book of Appreciative Inquiry by Sue Annis Hammon or visit **www.connection.cwru.edu/ai**.

CHARRETTE: A Charrette is a community planning process that helps large, diverse groups undertake an urban design project rapidly and collaboratively. It takes its name from a French cart used centuries ago by architecture students to rush their design drawings to Paris's Ecole des Beaux Arts. Charrettes engage a large, diverse group of community members along side professional planners and architects so that professionals can help lay people express their own vision, preferences and desired outcomes for a project, neighborhood or whole city using a variety of design tools.

> A charrette condenses the process of going back and forth between public hearings and professional design work into one intense session.

This process can range from multi-day sessions involving lots of technical equipment and professionals (the new urbanist model) to a more modest one to two day session with some professional help, and maps, pens and flipcharts rather than computers (the design workshop model). All variations are focused on engaging community members in designing their own futures in a very graphic, tangible, and hands-on manner. Professionals are there to assist people to articulate, visualize and see the potential outcomes of their own ideas and desires, not to develop the design themselves. Large groups are broken up into teams, which present their ideas to the larger group. More work is done in areas where group agreement is growing. This structure condenses the arduous process of going back and forth between public hearings and professional design work into one intense session, meanwhile building community support.

The American Institute of Architects (AIA)has a program called Regional Urban Design Assistance Team (RUDAT) which can work with qualified communities to do three day charrette processes. Visit **www.aia.org/rudat**.

For more information consult: W. L. Riddick, <u>Charrette Processes: a tool in urban planning</u>, or visit **www.charretteinsitute.org**.

Great Meetings!

great results

Chapter Six
Choosing the Right Tool

THIS CHAPTER DESCRIBES A NUMBER OF BASIC TOOLS TO HELP GROUPS THROUGH THE process steps described in *Chapter Five: Understanding Process*. To make it easier to photocopy, each tool starts on its own page and includes a brief description, an indication of when it is useful and, where appropriate, some cautions about the tool. There is an explanation of how to use the tool and, finally, an example.

This collection is not intended to be an encyclopedia of all the tools available. Every day we discover or invent new ones — and so will you. In the *Reading and Resources* section at the end of the book are some suggestions for additional reading, which will describe more tools.

Below is a list of the tools, grouped by process step, and in the order in which they appear in the following pages. In addition, the pages in this chapter are designed with a tab along the long edge to assist you in finding the right tools for the process steps of generating ideas, evaluating ideas, or deciding.

Generating Ideas	Evaluating Ideas	Deciding
BRAINSTORMING • popcorn • hybrid • one-at-a-time • sticky note • subgroup • subset • warm-up DEFINING AND ANALYZING A PROBLEM • brain mapping • fishbone diagram • picture it • SWOT analysis • what is/isn't the problem VISIONING THE IDEAL • wish, want, wonder • newspaper article about the future • picture the path to the future • defining the vision	CONSOLIDATING/ NARROWING • affinity groups • loop and group LISTING IN PRIORITY ORDER • multivote • pick 3 — drop 3 • nominal group technique • paired comparisons EVALUATING OPTIONS • option comparison grid • force field analysis • pro/con sheet	VOTING • voting: majority or supermajority CONSENSUS • levels of consensus • stoplight cards • thumbs up SENSE OF THE GROUP • sense of the group

Hints for Choosing the Right Tool

Every facilitator needs a set of tools and techniques in order to be able to suggest tools for groups to use in different situations. In selecting the most effective tool, you need to answer these questions:

1. What process step is the group in: defining the issue; envisioning the goal; or developing a solution/decision?

2. Are you trying to generate ideas, evaluate ideas or decide?

3. What other group factors are influencing the group: size of the group; the group's stage of development (i.e., forming, storming, norming, performing); energy of the group; introvert/extrovert mix in the group; group's ability to use the tool; power dynamics in the group; and whether the topic is highly conflictual.

Brainstorming and its Variations

Brainstorming is by now a familiar process to many groups. In general, it means a process that allows a group to generate a lot of ideas on a given topic without stopping to talk about or evaluate each idea as it is written down. There are many variations on brainstorming. Brainstorming is appropriate any time a group needs to come up with a list of ideas. Coming up with multiple ideas can be part of any process step whether analyzing an issue, envisioning the desired goal or working on a solution or decision.

When it is useful:

- to generate a list of problems or potential problems
- to generate a list of causes of problems
- to generate topics for data collection
- to generate a list of suggestions for what the ideal would look like
- to generate a list of potential solutions
- to generate a list of next steps

Rules for brainstorming:

- Express whatever comes to your mind. Don't monitor, censor, or hold back responses. The more ideas, the better. No idea is too far out.
- Do not evaluate your ideas or anybody else's ideas. Do not make positive evaluations, negative comments or non-verbal agreement or disagreement. It is especially important for the facilitator and recorder to refrain from giving any indication of evaluation.
- Do not discuss the ideas as they come up. Discussion will interfere with the generation of creative possibilities. Ask only essential questions about brainstorming items.
- Repetition of ideas is okay. Write down each idea, even if it sounds repetitious. There is no value in having a narrowed-down list at this point and people can feel rejected if their ideas aren't written down.

Brainstorming, Continued

- Piggy-backing on someone else's ideas should be encouraged. This is often the building block of workable solutions.
- Silence is normal in brainstorming. When it seems as though people have run out of ideas, restate the topic of brainstorming and then ask, "Anything else?" Wait 10 seconds or so; often after a period of silence there is a burst of creativity.

Hints for Brainstorming

- Review the rules for brainstorming every time you use this method.

- Set a time limit for brainstorming and stick to it.

- If you are looking to break out of customary ways of thinking, get people away from the table: have them sit in a circle of chairs around the easel or even on the floor in order to break out of customary ways of thinking.

- Affirm humor, laughter and anything creative.

- Summarize an idea and then check with the person to make sure you have understood correctly what he was saying.

- Be assertive in stopping any judgmental comments. Remind the evaluating person gently that right now the group is generating ideas, not evaluating them.

Popcorn Brainstorming

Popcorn brainstorming allows anyone to speak up at anytime until all the ideas are out. Although the process is very informal and unstructured, you will still want to be watching to see that everyone gets a chance to speak up and share ideas.

When it is useful:

- in a group that is ready with ideas and doesn't need any warm up or time to think about it
- in a group that works well together so that you are not concerned about uneven participation

How to use it:

1. Have enough space to accommodate lots of ideas. You can use flip chart, butcher paper, chalk board, white board or self-stick sheets.
2. Review the rules of brainstorming with the group. If the concept is unfamiliar to the group, post the rules on a sheet of paper.
3. Record all ideas that participants offer, being careful to model the above rules.
4. After you have finished brainstorming, ask the group to review each item for clarity and completeness.

Cautions:

Popcorn brainstorming does not work as well in groups with a high percentage of introverts, with one or more dominating personalities or with people who are too shy to get into the unstructured fray.

Example:

Your regular staff team is working on ways to reduce the steps needed to do a particular task. It is a small group that works well together and is full of ideas. You outline the purpose of the brainstorming for them. "Well, everyone is clear about the issue and the goal. Now it is time to generate all the creative ideas you can think of for ways to reduce the number of steps in accomplishing this task. You remember the rules of brainstorming. No discussion or evaluation of ideas as they go up. Questions and evaluation will come later. Remember to encourage everyone to share ideas. OK, who has an idea?" As each idea is presented you record it, summarizing if necessary. If the energy lags, encourage the group to generate even more. If you haven't heard from everyone, ask for thoughts from those who haven't a chance to speak up yet, without calling on people individually. When you think the group is done, do one last call for new ideas, before you move on to the evaluation phase.

Hybrid Brainstorming/Consensus Building

Hybrid Brainstorming/Consensus Building is a process that combines brainstorming with narrowing and decision making.

When it is useful:

- for creating ground rules
- whenever you want to end up with an agreed upon list

How to use it:

1. Any idea can be put on the table.
2. As each idea is suggested, the facilitator gets consensus from the group. The item is only written on the list after everyone agrees that it should be there.
3. It is important to reinforce and encourage the value of all offered ideas.

Example:

You are working with a newly formed group and you need to create ground rules. You want to be sure that everyone agrees to each ground rule before it gets written down, since it is hard to undo the legitimacy given to an idea that is written on the flipchart. "Now that we all know what ground rules are, let's create a list. What would be helpful to you or the group? We'll check each idea to see if everyone is comfortable with it before it goes up on the board." Vanessa suggests no side conversations. You check with the group. "Does everyone understand what no side conversations means? Does everyone feel comfortable with that as a ground rule or would anyone like to change or amend that before it goes up?" Seth voices a concern that he doesn't want to be reprimanded for asking his neighbor a quick question. You ask Seth what amendment might make it more acceptable to him and he suggests adding "other than quick questions." You check with the group. They readily agree and you add Seth's phrase, "no side conversations other than quick questions." You continue taking ideas and checking them.

Cautions:

It can be time consuming to stop over each idea. And if you are looking for lots of creative ideas, this method may dampen creativity by stopping and evaluating as you go along.

Note:

Since the ground rules belong to the whole group, everyone needs to agree to them. Through this method of brainstorming, the group ends up with the product it needs and does not have to do any further evaluating or selecting.

One-at-a-time Brainstorming

One-at-a-time brainstorming is a variation on brainstorming that provides individual thinking time. It encourages participation by getting everyone involved.

When it is useful:

- in groups with introverted members who are usually more comfortable developing ideas internally prior to speaking
- for groups with members who tend to dominate discussions
- for groups which need additional time to think about the questions

Cautions:

One-at-a-time brainstorming can be too slow-paced for some individuals or groups.

How to use it:

1. Each person, working individually, makes a list of ideas.
2. Ask each person in the group to read out one item on her list.
3. After one or two rounds of collecting ideas from individuals, open it up to regular brainstorming until all ideas have been shared. Opening it up keeps the process from becoming too tedious.
4. After all ideas have been shared, invite the group to add anything else it has thought of as the list was being created.

Example:

You are working with a newly formed group that includes a mix of extroverted and introverted people. You state the question of the brainstorm, "The task right now is to think of all the different ways this organization could increase its revenues. Take the next few minutes to make your own list of all the creative ideas you can think of, no matter how zany, for increasing revenues." After a few minutes, you begin recording ideas taking one at a time from each person. "So let's hear what people have come up with. I'll take one idea from each of you first and then we'll keep going around until everything is up on the flip chart. Remember to save your questions and comments on ideas until the next section of the agenda.

Sticky Note Brainstorming

In this brainstorming variation, group members write their brainstormed ideas on sticky notes, and then place the notes on a wall for everyone to see. The ideas are then grouped by topic or theme, providing a visual picture of which ideas are mentioned most often by the group.

When it is useful:

- when the group needs an exercise that will get them up and moving
- any time people would like some distance from the ideas they put up because it is a difficult subject or there is a power differential in the room that is making some people unwilling to speak
- if you want the ability to move ideas around or sort them

How to use it:

1. Give each person markers and several large sticky notes or cards (the larger the better). Ask participants to put one idea on each card. If you are seeking contrasting ideas, such as what works and what doesn't, provide different colored cards or sticky paper. Remind the group to write clearly and boldly so the ideas can be read from a distance.

2. If there are no concerns about anonymity, ask participants to stick their own cards on the wall.

3. If maintaining anonymity is an issue, collect the cards yourself and put them on the wall.

4. Ask participants to come up to the wall and read one another's cards.

5. At this point, you can move into the evaluation process step and ask the group to organize them in clumps of similar ideas, or you can group them yourself. The former provides for more involvement. However it requires that people are clear about how they are supposed to be organizing the information. See "Affinity Groups" on page 107 of this chapter.

Cautions:

The notes can become cumbersome and transcribing them at the end can be tricky. Also, you have to make sure that people write legibly.

Sticky Note Brainstorming, Continued

Example:

You are facilitating a meeting in an office where the staff has been having trouble getting along. You want to generate ideas on what might improve the working environment. It is a potentially touchy subject and you feel people may be reluctant to speak up. You pose the question to the group, "What ideas do you have about ways to improve the team work in our office? They could be on anything from the layout of the furniture to the way we communicate with one another. Take the next five minutes to list your ideas on the sticky notes that I have passed around. Please put just one idea per note and write legibly so that others will be able to read it. I'll come around and collect your notes and put them up on the board." After all the notes are up, ask the group to come up and help sort them out. "Now, everyone come up to the board. First, take the time to read everything that is up there. Next, you can move to the evaluation step by organizing the ideas in the categories that seem appropriate. Some ideas may be identical, others may not fit easily into any category and will need to stand on their own." When they have finished reading and organizing, help the group summarize what is on the board, "Well, it looks as if we have a large concentration of comments on communication issues ranging from not listening to using inflammatory words," etc.

Subgroup Brainstorming

Subgroup brainstorming divides the whole group into smaller groups. The task of each small group is to generate a list of ideas to be shared with the whole group. Working in smaller groups gives everyone more opportunity to participate and can be more comfortable for some.

When it is useful:

- when you have a large group and want to give everyone a chance to contribute in a short period of time
- when you have some dominating personalities in the group who are making it hard for quieter people to be heard
- when people are reluctant to speak up and feel safer having their ideas come from a group
- when you want to generate noise and energy in the room through multiple conversations

How to use it:

1. Divide a large group into subgroups of two to four participants. Give a time limit and ask each subgroup to choose a recorder/reporter.
2. Each subgroup generates a list of ideas.
3. For reporting out, take just one idea at a time from each group, moving from group to group.
4. After one or two rounds of collecting ideas from reporters, open it up to a regular brainstorming session until all ideas have been shared.
5. After all ideas have been shared, invite the group to add anything else it has thought of as the list was being created.

Cautions:

Some individuals may be uncomfortable not hearing all the conversations, especially if there is some mistrust in the group.

Example:

You have a group of 20 people who have been asked to come up with a list of ideas for streamlining the process for managing returns. It is a mixed group of team leaders and team members. Some are more outspoken than others, and some have reservations about speaking up in a large group. You decide to divide the group into subgroups of four people. "Our task today is to generate a list of suggestions for improving and streamlining the returns process. I'd like to have you get into groups

Subgroup Brainstorming, Continued

of four people to start your thinking and to generate a list of ideas on the flipchart to bring back to the full group." You can choose to have the groups gather as they are seated already. Or, if you want to mix people up, you can have them count off one to four, having the ones form a group, the twos form a group, and so on. "You have 15 minutes in your small group to come up with a list of ideas. I'll let you know when there are five minutes left. You don't have to agree on all the ideas, just collect a list to bring back to the full group." Make sure that each group has the supplies it needs to create its own list of ideas. When the groups are done, take one idea at a time from each group until all the ideas are listed.

Subset Brainstorming

Here the facilitator invites brainstorming ideas from different perspectives: frivolous, serious, boring, funny, etc. This kind of "thinking outside the box" helps groups get their creative juices flowing. Sometimes unusual ideas can turn out to be more practical than they might seem at first.

When it is useful:

- when a group needs to be creative
- when a group is stuck or just bored with regular brainstorming

How to use it:

1. Encourage the group to generate ideas "outside the box" of sensible ideas. Remind them that putting out an idea is different from thinking it is necessarily good or workable.
2. As the group is brainstorming, challenge them with subsets for brainstorming (e.g. practical solutions, boring solutions, improbable solutions, extravagant, funny solutions, etc.). You might say something like, "Those were great practical solutions, now how about all the silly solutions you can think of."
3. Follow the steps for regular brainstorming.

Cautions:

Individuals may be uncomfortable being associated with their silly ideas. If this seems to be a concern, collect ideas on sticky notes or index cards.

Example:

Your regular staff team is working on ways to reduce the use of office supplies. It is a small group that has a tendency to get stuck in old, familiar thinking and you would like to push for something more innovative. You outline the purpose of the brainstorming for them, "Well, everyone is clear about the issue and the goal. Now it is time to generate all the creative ideas we can think of for ways to reduce the use of office supplies. You remember the rules of brainstorming. No discussion or evaluation of ideas as they go up. Questions and evaluation will come later. Remember to encourage everyone to share ideas. OK, who has an idea?" As each idea is presented, you record it, summarizing if necessary. Since you are both facilitating and participating, remember to add your own ideas, too. Next, challenge them to think of silly solutions. "We've created a good start here with some practical ideas. Now, try to think of some ridiculous solutions. Don't worry about being far out." When the

Subset Brainstorming, Continued

group has generated additional ideas, ask them to look at the new list to see if some of the silly ideas actually suggest a workable solution for reducing the amount of office supplies used.

Warm-up Brainstorming

Warm-up brainstorming uses a topic that is non-task related to warm up the group. It helps a group loosen up and demonstrates the creative solutions possible in brainstorming.

When it is useful:

- when your group needs to loosen up to be creative
- when your group is taking itself too seriously or is stuck in the status quo
- as an icebreaker

<u>Cautions:</u>

Participants may be reluctant at first to do something that seems to be unrelated to the task at hand.

How to use it:

1. Show any object (soda bottle, lint brush, etc.) and ask the group to brainstorm all possible uses.
   Or give the group an imaginary situation and ask them to brainstorm all possible solutions. For example, "You're in Mexico on vacation and all your credit cards, money and passport have been stolen. How are you going to get home?"
2. Follow the steps for brainstorming.

Example:

You have a group of 20 people who have been asked to come up with a list of ideas for improving the process for managing returns. The participants have been working in returns, using the same process, for a long time. You are concerned that it will be hard for them to see any other way of doing the task. "Our task today is to generate a list of suggestions for improving and streamlining the returns process. But, before we go to the returns process itself, let's do a little warm up exercise for creative problem solving. Imagine that you have to move a seventy-five pound box of glass bottles of beer from one warehouse room to another. You have one helper, two rolling pins, ten feet of light rope and a balloon. How many different ways could you move that box?" Let people work in small groups to generate more energy and ideas. Encourage them to be silly or far-fetched in their ideas. Give the groups five or ten minutes and let them report back to each other encouraging their imagination and humor. When they are done, congratulate them on their innovative solutions. Relate the variety of ideas they just generated to the need for a variety of solutions in the returns process. Then, start on the real task of ways to improve the returns process using the variation on brainstorming that will serve the group best.

Brain/Mind Mapping

Brain mapping is a graphic way to display the analysis of different parts of a problem or issue. The main problem or issue is placed in a central circle and the causes of the problem are represented as separate spokes or circles attached to the central circle. There can be more detail attached to any of the causes with additional spokes or circles.

When it is useful:

- to break down a problem, showing the causes and the subsets of those causes in relationship to one another
- to analyze an issue whether you are looking for the causes or trying to understand all the parts of an issue
- to break out the pieces of a task or the steps in reaching an outcome or goal
- to follow the consequences of an action and analyze whether there might be unintended consequences
- to generate a graphic display for clarity

Cautions:

Brain mapping can result in too much detail and it is easy to get sidetracked on debates over placement. It needs to be rewritten to be useful.

How to use it for analyzing a problem or brainstorming:

1. At the center of your paper, draw a circle with the problem written in the middle.
2. Draw spokes out from the center on which you write the causes of the problem.
3. As participants further define each cause, add the ideas on spokes attached to the cause spokes.

Brain Mapping, Continued

Example:

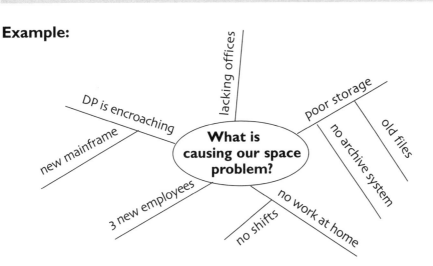

How to use it for the consequences of an action:

1. Write the action in a circle.
2. Put the consequences of that action in circles attached to the original circle.
3. As those consequences have further consequences, attach more circles to them.

Example:

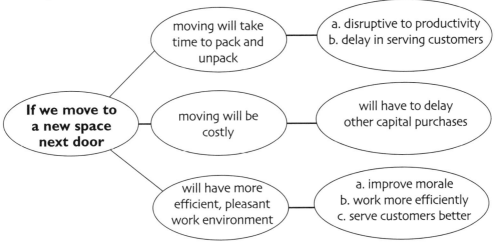

Fishbone Diagram

The fishbone diagram is similar to brain mapping. It is a graphic way to tease apart the elements of an issue or problem. It can examine the causes of a problem or the implications of a decision.

When it is useful:

- to break down a problem, showing the causes and the subsets of those causes in relationship to one another
- to analyze an issue whether you are looking for the causes or trying to understand all the parts of an issue
- to break out the pieces of a task or the steps in reaching an outcome or goal
- to follow the consequences of an action and analyze whether there might be unintended consequences

Cautions:

Fishbone Diagram can result in too much detail and it is easy to get sidetracked on debates over placement. It also needs to be rewritten to be useful.

How to use it for analyzing a problem or looking at consequences:

1. At the right hand edge of your paper, draw a triangle in the rough shape of a fish head with the problem written in the middle.
2. Draw a horizontal line from the center of the fish head to the left edge of the paper as if it were a back bone.
3. As people identify different causes or consequences put them on lines drawn off of the back bone as if they were ribs.
4. As participants further define each cause or consequence, add the ideas on lines attached to the appropriate ribs.

Fishbone Diagram, Continued

Example:

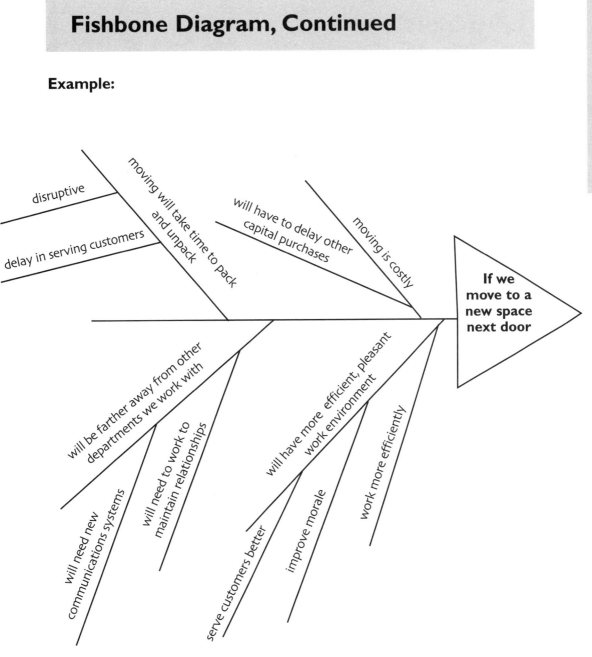

Picture It

Drawing an image of a problem, issue or organizational structure gives people a different, creative way to express something that may be hard to put in words.

When it is useful:

- to help define a situation which is hard to put into words
- to capture people's feeling about a situation
- when the group is stuck and needs a fresh approach
- to add energy to a group or provide a non-verbal outlet for expression

Cautions:

You may need to reassure participants that this exercise is not about creating art; it is about expressing ideas in a different way.

How to use it:

1. Divide the group into teams of two to four people so that they can share ideas and help each other.
2. Ask each group to create an image that expresses the situation that you are trying to define. The image can be literal, figurative or metaphorical.
3. Reassure them that drawing talent doesn't matter. This is not an art class. Whatever they come up with is fine.
4. Supply the groups with flipchart paper (full or half size sheets) and plenty of pens in different colors.
5. When they are done, display the "posters" and ask each group to explain its image.
6. Summarize by checking with the group about what they learned and how they see the situation differently now.

Example:

Your group is working on the organizational structure of their large and complex department. They have been stuck in the status quo and can't seem to describe what the problem is. You divide the group into teams of three people each and ask them to develop an image, "Think about the structure and organization of our department. How would you describe it graphically? What image comes to your mind as you think about it? It could be anything from a traditional organizational plan to an image that is a metaphor for what it feels like. Discuss ideas in your group and come

Picture It, Continued

up with one or more images and draw them for the rest of the group. You have 20 minutes to generate your image. Then we will take a look at every group's poster. Identify someone in the group the report back to the whole group." After the posters are up, you ask each reporter to explain the group's image. "Tell us about your image and why it describes the department's structure for you." After all the images have been explained, you check for people's reactions, "So, what did you learn about the department in this exercise? What new insights did the process of developing your own image or seeing other images give you?"

SWOT Analysis

SWOT (Strengths, Weaknesses, Opportunities and Threats) analysis is a tool for analyzing the current situation both internally (strengths and weaknesses) and externally (opportunities and threats). It provides helpful baseline information for a group that wants to vision the future or analyze a problem.

When it is useful:

- to help a group determine where it stands and what it might need to work on in order to get to where it wants to go
- as part of the background analysis for solving a problem

How to use it:

1. For strengths, ask the group to look at those activities that it does very well, at the skills of the group or of individuals within the group, at valuable experience, at the depth of its work force or the quality of its leadership. List their ideas on flip chart paper. It is important that enough safety and openness has been created in the process so that responses are candid. Record their responses.
2. For weaknesses, ask the group to consider and list the same wide range of possibilities. Again, candor is important. Some agreement on the items raised is helpful, but this is usually a step in a longer planning process, not an end in itself.
3. Ask the group to identify opportunities — the external factors that could be used to the benefit of the group. They could be in the form of funding sources, marketing possibilities, disarray in the competition, a favorable political climate or public awareness. These are events or circumstances over which the group has no control, but which will help the group go where it wants to go.
4. Ask the group to identify and list the threats — those negative possibilities that might trip the group up, or the storm clouds on the horizon that might necessitate changing course.
5. You can use any form of generating ideas (see tools for Brainstorming) and identifying some group agreement (see tools for Evaluating and Deciding).

SWOT Analysis, Continued

Example:

Strengths • board members are deeply committed to agency • staff has culture of collaboration • agency has excellent reputation for high quality services	**Opportunities** • growing economy • influx of affluent retirees, money and volunteerism • opportunity for mergers
Weaknesses • lack of financial reserves • multiple offices in dispersed locations • more communication and efficiency difficulty	**Threats** • tax payer revolt underway • too many social service agencies — we get lost in the mix

INTERNAL

EXTERNAL

What Is/Isn't the Problem

What is/isn't the problem is a method for narrowing the focus onto the true problem or issue.

When it is useful:

- to help a group identify a problem precisely

How to use it:

1. Define the overall problem area. For example: The lack of quality play equipment in the neighborhood playground.
2. Make one list that indicates what is the problem and a second list of what is not the problem.
3. It is best to put both lists up at the same time — either using two sheets of flip chart paper or two sections of a white board or chalkboard. Then you can record whatever ideas people come up with.

Example:

Why do we have a lack of quality playground equipment in the neighborhood?

WHAT IS THE PROBLEM	WHAT ISN'T THE PROBLEM
• lack of federal, state or municipal funds for purchase of equipment	• the willingness of city director of parks and recreation to accept suggestions for improvement
• lack of city personnel to maintain the equipment	• lack of families that use the playground
• low priority of this playground relative to other playgrounds in the city	• individuals in the neighborhood who are willing to give their time and energy to upgrade the park

Wish, Want, Wonder

This tool provides a method for encouraging a group to frame the situation positively and focus on the way they want things to be. By asking the participants to use phrases such as "I wish, I want, I wonder if we could, I wonder how we could…" you encourage group members to state what they would like to see rather than being bogged down in problems.

When it is useful:

- to move a group beyond complaining about what is wrong and get focused more positively
- to spur creativity, fresh thinking or a more constructive approach

Cautions:

This exercise may seem disconnected from reality for some participants.

How to use it:

1. Ask people to generate options by phrasing statements that begin with either "I wish," "I wonder," "how to" or "what if."
2. Help participants reframe their concerns into positive statements about the way they want it to be.
3. Capture their "wishes" on the board.

Example:

Your United Way committee is charged with planning next year's Day of Caring program. The group is discouraged by last year's turnout and complains about everything that went wrong. You want them to describe what they want more constructively. You ask them to brainstorm about next year's program using phrases that start with "I wish". For example, "I wish we could double the number of participants." The group gets started, but Tanya persists in complaining about last year's poor publicity. Gently you encourage her, "Tanya, what do you wish next year's publicity would be like?", so that you can shift her focus back to the future and the desired outcome.

Newspaper Article About the Future

Writing a newspaper article, which reports on the organization or situation as the group would like it to be in the future, is a way of capturing the group's concepts of the desired future and building a belief in how it could be.

When it is useful:

- to establish a vision of the future
- to build a belief in the possible and generate enthusiasm
- to provide inspiration and/or summary for a group

How to use it:

1. Ask the group members to picture themselves and their organization a few years in the future. The organization is running well. What would they hope to see reported in the newspaper about them or what would a major news magazine be saying about them?
2. Let them brainstorm a list of ideas or comments that they would want to have in the article. Look for agreement on the key ideas. Then, have the group work on a headline for the article, using small groups to come up with ideas. Generate agreement around one or two headlines.
3. If you are in a process that includes a subsequent meeting, ask for some volunteers to actually write an article based on the group's ideas and then bring it back to the group at the next meeting.
4. In preparation for strategic planning and visioning, you could ask each member of the group to write his own article and share it with the group.

Example:

You are working with an organization that has been having difficulty with its public image. Bickering among board members and difficulties with the previous director have created negative feelings in the community. The group wants to develop a plan to improve the working relationships within the board and with

Newspaper Article, Continued

the staff, and to improve the organization's public image. They are having trouble imagining the way they want the relationships to be. You ask them to picture themselves two years in the future in a smoothly running organization, "A reporter from the local paper has done a feature article on your organization. What does the article say? What are the key ideas that it conveys? What activities does it report on? What kind of vocabulary does she use to describe the organization and its activities? What does she say about the Board meeting that she attends?" Ask them to work in pairs or small groups to generate ideas. Collect the ideas and look for agreement on key themes, ideas and vocabulary. Next, ask the group to work in their pairs or small groups again to come up with a great headline for the article, based on the ideas that the group just agreed to. Again, bring the ideas together and look for agreement on one or two headlines, or a new one encompassing several of the ideas. If your group will be meeting again, ask for two to three volunteers to actually write up the article, to be shared with the group next time.

Picture the Path to the Future

Picture the path to the future is a graphic way of capturing the group's concepts of the future and a sense of movement toward that goal by using a drawing and symbolic representations of ideas.

When it is useful:

- to establish a vision of the future, a path to get there and a view of the present
- to create a graphic display of ideas which may help some people in the group understand it more clearly
- to sketch the larger concepts and ideas
- to provide inspiration and excitement for a group
- to provide clarity and summary of ideas

Cautions:

This tool does not provide a detailed plan for how to achieve a goal.

How to use it:

1. Attach a large, preferably horizontal piece of paper to the wall. Set up a basic scene with an outline of mountains and a road running from the foreground to the pass between the mountains.
2. Ask your group to describe the present situation and put it in the foreground at the beginning of the road. Along the road put the steps needed to get to the desired future. In the sky over the mountains capture the goals or ideals.

Example:

Defining the Vision

Defining the vision is a technique to help the participants paint a picture in their minds. It gives participants a chance to "see" the details, which then help them articulate their vision of the way they want things to be.

When it is useful:

- to identify what they would like to see in the future
- to collect ideas in a very open way
- to help participants focus on the future or the intangible

How to use it:

1. Create a scene for the group (often of an ideal or changed scenario) by leading the group through a visualization where they have the ability to see from the vantage point of a hot air balloon or some imaginary point. If it is important to consider particular facets of the organization's future, ask participants to do so.
2. Ask people to notice what they see, hear and feel.
3. Give participants a moment to make notes about what they have seen.
4. If the group is large (more than eight), break up into small groups. This will give individuals a chance to talk and generate more ideas in less time.
5. Pull the whole group together and gather the ideas. Take one idea from one small group and check to see if other groups dealt with that idea as well. Look for the sense of the whole group before you write up that element of the vision. Then move on to the next group for an idea and check that with the group as a whole. Continue around all the groups, checking each element of the future vision with the full group before you add it to the summary. Look for areas of agreement and areas of differences that need to be worked out. By the end, you should have a list of the key elements of the vision that reflects the sense of the whole group.

Cautions:

Defining a vision generates quite varied ideas which can make summarizing a challenge. And for some the "close your eyes and imagine" approach may feel either uncomfortable or difficult.

Defining the Vision, Continued

Example:

Ask participants to close their eyes and imagine with you. "It is now five years in the future and your organization is functioning beautifully, just the way you would like it to be. You have special powers to view your organization. You can fly to any height and can see the town or the whole state in a glance. You also have x-ray vision and enhanced hearing. What do you see, hear and feel? Whom is the organization serving? What is the structure of the organization? What kind of facilities is it operating in? What is the tone and content of the conversation on message boards, or in the lunch room?" You can highlight whatever is important for the group to focus on.

Affinity Groups

This tool uses sticky note brainstorming (see page 85) with a particular method for consolidating the ideas. It enables the group to decide how the ideas should be organized.

When it is useful:

- to group a number of ideas in themes or categories
- for a large group in which you want everyone to participate
- to move fairly quickly with no debating
- to provide an opportunity to get up and move around

How to use it:

1. Have each participant put his ideas on sticky notes or cards with only one idea per note and stick them on the wall using thumbtacks, masking tape, adhesive paper, etc.
2. When all the ideas are on the wall, invite the group members to reorder the ideas into groups of similar ideas without talking. Each member is free to move any idea and the process continues in silence until no one wants to make any further moves.
3. Invite the group to discuss their choices and check for agreement.

Cautions:

People do not have a chance to explain the reasons for their moves. The notes can become cumbersome and transcribing them at the end can be tricky. Legible handwriting is a must.

Note:

This technique can be used with or without the "no talking" rule.

Example:

Your group wants to identify ways to improve inter-departmental communications. Each person puts on the wall as many ideas as he has from "start a newsletter" to "hold monthly department meetings." Members then read all the ideas and begin silently to group them. A group of ideas around newsletters and written communications emerges. Another forms around physical rearrangement, and another around meetings. One person may create a grouping that others don't agree with and the ideas get moved again. When everyone is either comfortable with the results or runs out of steam, the group sits down and discusses what it has created.

Evaluating Ideas → Narrowing

Loop and Group

This is a technique for helping a group to consolidate ideas after a brainstorming session by grouping similar items. By circling in one color items that are similar or belong to a common theme, you can visually link common ideas and reduce the number of items under consideration.

When it is useful:

- to bring order to a random collection of ideas
- to start the narrowing process

How to use it:

1. Use questions to the group to solicit their opinions on what belongs together or, if it would help the group, reflect what you see as similarities. Some questions that you might ask are: "Are some of these items really the same issue? Are some of these items part of a single larger issue? What would you call that larger topic? What is the title? Are there any items which do not belong on the list of this topic?"
2. Circle or underline the ideas belonging to one group using the same color marker.
3. Using a different color, circle the ideas that belong to another group.
4. If the original list, with its multi-colored circles, is getting hard to read, you may want to create a new list of the titles of the new, larger topic areas.

Example:

Your group has generated twenty different ideas on how to improve the parking situation at your work place. You ask if any of the ideas are similar or belong in the same category. The group decides that four of the ideas have to do with ways to reorganize the parking spaces in the parking lot. You circle those four ideas with a purple pen. Next someone suggests that several of the ideas are really alternatives to driving your own car to work. The group agrees and you circle those ideas in green. You continue in this way until the list is organized into a number of manageable areas. If the original sheet with the 20 ideas is now hard to read, or the titles of the new groupings are not clear, make a new sheet with the titles of the topic areas and identify the color of the topic's "loops."

Multivoting

Multivoting is a process for narrowing down a larger list of items and indicating a group's interest or priority in each item.

When it is useful:

- to narrow a list, as long as it is acceptable that some items may drop off completely
- to get a "quick read" on a group's priorities

How to use it:

1. Make sure there is clarity about the meaning of each item on the list. Where there is agreement to do so, combine like ideas.
2. Be clear, too, about the criteria group members should use to make their choices. Depending on the situation, it might be "items that will have the strongest impact on revenue," or "items that I have a real commitment to make happen."
3. The N/3 (N over 3) method is a good way to determine how many votes group members should get. N equals the number of items on the list; divide that number by 3.
4. Everyone gets the same number of votes. Members can cast votes by making marks on the flipchart, by a show of hands or secret ballot. A benefit of marking the flipchart is that people can get up and move around, which often raises the energy level in the group.
5. Clearly describe the method for vote distribution. There are two common ways for individuals to distribute their votes. One way is to agree that no item on the list can get more than one vote from one person. For example, if group members each have 5 votes, they would vote on 5 different items. The second way is to agree that an individual can distribute his votes however he chooses, putting all votes on one item, or distributing them in any other way among multiple items. If each group member had five votes, he could put all five votes on one item,

Cautions:

Multivoting is not appropriate when the group needs to consider carefully each item on a list and/or when it needs to incorporate each idea into a final recommendation. Multivoting should not be used as a way to avoid conflict or circumvent an important, but perhaps difficult, discussion.

Note:

The method that permits people to stack their votes can create results which are not reflective of the majority of the group.

Evaluating Ideas → Listing by Priority

Multivoting, Continued

one vote on five different items, etc.

6. Once the votes are tallied, be clear about what happens to all the items on the list. Don't assume that those items that received fewer votes should be cast aside. Sometimes the group will want to save them, or include them in a report.

Example:

Your group has generated a list of 25 different projects that individual partici-pants want the team to undertake this year. Since there are many more projects than can be done during the year and more than you have time to discuss thor-oughly in the meeting, you would like to know which projects hold the most interest for the group overall. Then you can focus the discussion on those items. You ask the group to select a short list of projects (usually the total number of items divided by three) based on clear, specific criteria. "You have created a great list of ideas. Let's see which ideas the group wants to focus on. Review the list and identify the eight projects that you think would be most important for the team to work on this year." You tally their votes using any of the methods in number four above and then check the result with the group. "It looks as if these five projects have significantly more votes than the others. Does it make sense to you that the team should focus its discussion on these five ideas?"

Pick 3 — Drop 3

Pick3 — Drop 3, a tool brought to our attention by James E. Moody, is a variation on multivoting which allows the group to shorten a brainstormed list by identifying both the highest and lowest priorities of the group. Some people find it easier to identify what should come off the list, while others are more comfortable identifying what to keep. This method accommodates both styles. It may not provide the final answer but it will provide an easier list to work with for a variety of other evaluative or decision making tools.

When it is useful:

- to narrow a list more quickly than by Multivoting
- to identify highest and/or lowest priorities of a list

How to use it:

1. Ask the members of the group to review the items on the list and select three that they believe should stay on the list for consideration. Those items should be highlighted with a checkmark or green colored dot.
2. Next, participants should select three items from the list that they think should be deleted. Those items should be distinguished in a different way, such as an "X" or a red colored dot.
3. Review the results of the marks with the group. Ask the participants if they agree that the items with the most Xs should be taken off the list. Strike off the items that the group agrees to remove.
4. If the list is long, you can repeat the process and take more items off the list with the group's agreement.
5. Identify the items with the largest number of positive votes, as you would in a standard Multivoting process.
6. Once the list is narrowed down to 2-6 items, you can use any of a number of evaluative tools to determine the best idea from the group. See the list of evaluation tools at the beginning of this chapter.

Example:

You have had a lively and imaginative brainstorming session on how to generate more name recognition for your small, social service organization. The group has generated 20 ideas ranging from regular press releases to sponsoring a bungee jump-

Pick 3 — Drop 3, Continued

ing festival in the main square, downtown. You need to shorten the list by identifying the most and least workable ideas so that you can do a more detailed comparison of the key possibilities. You ask the group to read the whole list and then put red dots by the three ideas they think should be dropped from the list and green dots by the three ideas that they think should definitely be kept on the list. The marks show that everyone agrees that the bungee jumping should be dropped and six other ideas have more than one red dot. The group agrees to take those seven ideas off the list. Next you look at the green dots and find that they are clustered around eight different ideas. There are no votes for the remaining items. You check with the group about choosing those eight items to explore further, and they agree. At this point, you suggest using Nominal Group Technique to give the group a more thorough discussion of the remaining eight items.

Nominal Group Technique

Nominal Group Technique is a narrowing and decision making method that allows for input by all group members while minimizing group debate.

When it is useful:

- to provide opportunity for people to share their reasons for their choices and to sway one another's thinking in a timely manner
- to avoid getting into debates or power struggles
- to manage strong differences in values

How to use it:

1. Each person individually decides his order of preference for the options given. Each option is ranked (first choice is one, second choice is two, etc.).
2. For each option, ask for input from someone who felt that the option should be a high priority. Others may add if they have an additional reason supporting the high priority designation or if they want to argue that it should be a low priority, but there is no general discussion.
3. Group members have a chance to change their order of preference based on the comments given.
4. The facilitator records each person's order of preference on a prepared flipchart.
5. Scores are tallied for each option.
6. Remember if people put one for their highest priority, two for their second and so on, whichever option gets the least number of points is the highest priority.
7. As with any decision making method, the group should look at the results and check that they make sense and are in line with the group's goals, resources, etc.

Evaluating Ideas → Listing by Priority

Nominal Group Technique, Continued

Example:

	Option A	Option B	Option C
Graham	2	1	3
Ian	2	3	1
Emily	1	3	2
Natalie	1	2	3
Total	6	9	9

Paired Comparisons

Based on a group decision making process, ISM, developed by John Warfield and written about and utilized by Carl Moore and Roberta Miller, Paired Comparisons is a method of establishing a prioritized list through a thorough debate of the items. It is done by discussing and then voting on pairs of items to determine which is a higher priority until you have established the relative importance of all the items.

When it is useful:

- to create a thoroughly debated prioritized list and give individuals an opportunity to argue for what is important to them
- to prioritize items which are not easily related to one another (apples and oranges, road repairs and rose gardens)
- when making "politically" difficult decisions
- to determine the highest priorities for funding when the budget is limited
- to provide order to the potentially messy problem of prioritizing options

Cautions:

The items being prioritized need to be clearly defined and agreed upon, and it is difficult to use this tool with a long list of options. It can be time consuming to debate each pair.

Evaluating Ideas → Listing by Priority

How to use it:

1. Make sure the items to be prioritized are clear and that the list is not too long (no more than six to seven items).
2. Try to anticipate how much debate there is likely to be. How contentious is the subject matter? How significant is the impact of the result on the people in the room? How complex are the issues? Set your time frame accordingly.
3. In advance, make a card for each item to be prioritized, which is large enough to be readable by the entire group. The placards will need to be moved during the process, so have tape, adhesive paper and other necessary equipment handy.
4. Create an area on the wall for the pair of items under discussion. Write "is a higher priority than" in the middle and leave space above and below for placards.
5. Begin by comparing item A and B. Place the placard for item A over the phrase "is a higher priority than" and the placard for item B below. It now reads "Item A is a higher priority than item B."
6. Ask if the participants agree or disagree with the statement and why. Allow a

Paired Comparisons, Continued

thorough debate and when the group is ready, call for a simple vote. Is item A a higher priority than item B? Everyone must vote one way or the other. If the vote is yes, then place A over B on the priority ladder.

7. Now introduce item C. Is C a higher priority than B? (Move the B placard back to the comparison side for the discussion.) Again, encourage a discussion and call for a vote. If the vote is yes, then C belongs higher than B in the priority ladder. Now you need to know if C is a higher priority than A, so you set up that comparison and repeat the process of discussion and voting. If the vote is yes, then C moves above A on the ladder.

8. Continue to introduce new items starting in the middle of the priority ladder, repeating the process of discussion and voting. If it is a lower priority than the item it is compared with, then move to the next item down the ladder for your next comparison. If it is a higher priority, then move to the next item up the ladder. Continue until all the items have been introduced and found their resting places. The result is a completely prioritized list.

Example:

You have three requests for capital expenditures for your department: a new carpet ($4000); a telephone and voice mail upgrade ($10,000); and two new computer stations ($12,000). You need to prioritize these capital requests to see where the limited money should go. Set up your placards on the wall and begin the comparisons:

First Round:	Second Round:	Third Round:
(A) carpet is a higher priority than (B) telephone. Discussion, vote — no.	(C) computer is a higher priority than (B) telephone. Discussion, vote — no.	(C) computer is a higher priority than (A) carpet. Discussion, vote — yes.
Priority Ladder (B) telephone (A) carpet	Priority Ladder (B) telephone (C) computer (A) carpet	Priority Ladder (B) telephone (C) computer (A) carpet

Option Comparison Grid

The Option Comparison Grid is a narrowing and decision making technique for comparing options against a set of criteria. Some examples of comparisons are: candidates for a job, different brands of a product, types of awards, etc.

When it is useful:

• to evaluate multiple options against a set of criteria in order to decide on the best option

How to use it:

1. Develop a set of criteria that the final choice must meet. Because options that don't meet these criteria will be tossed out, make sure that these criteria are critical.
2. Develop a second set of criteria that would add value to the final choice.
3. List the options across the top of the chart.
4. Compare each option to each "must" criteria.
5. If an option does not meet a "must" criteria, toss it out. There is no need to continue the comparison for that option.
6. Compare each option that has met all the "must" criteria to the "add value" criteria. Write in any relevant comments.
7. After comparing all the options, assess which one best meets your set of criteria.
8. As always in a decision making process, ask if the final result makes sense. If some group members express hesitations about the choice, probe that discomfort to see if some criteria have been missed or over- or under-valued.

Evaluating Ideas → Evaluating Options

Option Comparison Grid, Continued

Example:

Hire New Marketing Director

"Must" Criteria	Candidate A	Candidate B	Candidate C
1. 5+ yrs. management	yes	yes	yes
2. MBA degree	yes	yes	no
3. Budget management	yes	yes	yes
4. Knows our software	yes	yes	yes
Added Value Criteria			
1. PR experience	yes	no	n/a
2. Media buying exper.	no	yes	n/a
3. Knowledge of industry	yes	no	n/a
4. Team leadership	yes	yes	n/a
Comments:	• Brother of CEO • Knows PR • Strong team leadership	• Seems like a a good fit • Knows media • Can't start for 6 mos.	• Has relevant industry experience • Requires high salary

Overall, which meets criteria best? Candidate A

Force Field Analysis

Force Field Analysis, as defined here, is a tool for assessing the forces that can work either for or against a particular change. It is a diagnostic management technique developed by Kurt Lewin, a pioneer in the field of social sciences. Lewin assumes that in any situation there are both driving and restraining forces that influence any change that may occur. This tool displays those forces graphically.

When it is useful:

- to articulate and analyze the factors that push a group toward, and restrain them from, making a particular change

How to use it:

1. Create a chart as shown in the example.
2. At the top of the chart, write a clear statement of the specific action you want to take. Use language that frames the change positively rather than negatively.
3. Using hybrid brainstorming to get agreement as you go along, brainstorm the specific factors (personal, situational, organizational, etc.) that could help you to move toward this desired outcome and write them on the chart. Then, brainstorm the specific factors that could work against reaching this desired outcome and write them on the chart. Remember to assess the situation from the perspective of all stakeholders.
4. Circle two or three driving forces you can increase the strength of, and two or three restraining forces of which you can minimize the impact.
5. List some steps you can take to increase the strength or decrease the impact of each driving or restraining force you have circled.

Force Field Analysis, Continued

Example:

Statement: We want to increase the number of Information Systems staff with Advanced Level Training Certificates (ALTC).

Driving Forces	Restraining Forces
Factors that work toward our goal	Factors that work against our goal
Company reimburses 100% of ALTC cost upon completion of training	Employee has to pay for ALTC course up front
ALTC qualifies employee for a pay grade increase	Employees attend training on their own time
Sense of satisfaction at new learning	Pay grade increase is dependent on appropriate job openings
ALTC is nationally recognized and therefore transferable to any work-place	Courses are offered just twice a year

Pro/Con Sheet

A pro/con sheet is a simple way to identify the reasons for and against a particular idea. It is a good way to look at all the aspects of an option before you decide whether or not to go forward.

When it is useful:

- to decide whether or not to go forward when the group is focused on a single option

How to use it:

1. Set up a chart with the "pros" on one side and the "cons" on the other. You can use two flip charts side by side or one sheet divided in half with a line. State the question clearly at the top.
2. Invite people's opinions as in regular brainstorming. You can record all the pros, then all the cons. If you are unsure if a comment is in favor or against, just ask.
3. After all the ideas are collected, check with the group to see if there are any comments that require clarification or further discussion. Look for the sense of the whole group in areas of disagreement.
4. Check with the group to see what conclusion they draw from the exercise and if they are ready to make a decision on the question.
5. Use the decision method that the group has agreed to.

Example:

The office that handles license fees, taxes and parking tickets needs to decide whether or not it should change from a standard 8:30 am to 5:00 pm day or go to a flexible schedule with people on different shifts between 7:30 am and 6:00 pm.

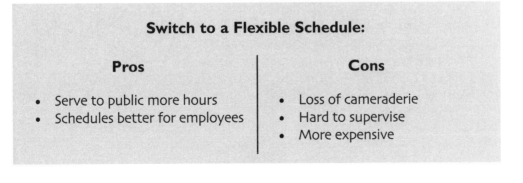

Switch to a Flexible Schedule:

Pros	Cons
• Serve to public more hours	• Loss of cameraderie
• Schedules better for employees	• Hard to supervise
	• More expensive

Evaluating Ideas → Evaluating Options

Voting

Voting is a time honored, democratic way of deciding issues in groups. It has the advantage of being clear and final (unless there is a tie). For many issues, it will be the simplest, quickest way to decide a matter. If your group wants to make sure that there is a high level of agreement, you can choose a higher threshold for passage than 51%, for example, two-thirds (66%) or three-quarters (75%).

When it is useful:

- when the issue requires a quick, definitive answer
- when the vote is not likely to create disaffected losers
- where participants are required by law to cast a vote (town councils, boards of directors, and so on)

How to use it:

1. Be sure that the question to be voted on is clearly stated.
2. Check to make sure that the group agrees that all the discussion is finished.
3. Call for the vote. You can use a simple show of hands. Or, if the matter is touchy or emotionally charged so that anonymity would be helpful, use paper ballots. Report the result to the group and check to make sure that it meets the pre-determined threshold.

Cautions:

Because voting is a win-lose process, it can cause disaffected losers who will not be committed to the implementation of the result. Relationships can suffer if a vote divides the group members.

Example:

Your group is moving quickly through a series of agreements around the location, refreshments and entertainment for the holiday party. After generating and evaluating ideas for each issue you call for a show of hands to see if you have the agreed upon two-thirds of the group in favor of the suggestion.

Levels of Consensus

Consensus is a form of decision making which is concluded only when all participants agree. It does not mean that everyone in the group loves the idea; only that
everyone in the group agrees to live with it and help to implement it. Levels of
Consensus is a decision making method which streamlines the consensus process.
Consensus-based groups often "talk an issue to death" as they struggle for unity.
This tool provides a format for checking consensus without all the long speeches
and discussions that can make consensus difficult. This method shortens the time
consensus can take and gives everyone a voice, without compromising the careful
listening, reflection, respect and trust that must accompany the use of consensus.

When it is useful:

- when the group appears to be close to a conclusion, but it is not apparent where
  everyone stands on the issue
- when 100% buy in is critical to the success of the issue

How to use it:

1. After the group has had sufficient time for discussion about a particular topic,
   ask all group members to hold up fingers indicating where they are on the consensus scale (see the Levels of Consensus on the following page). If a quick scan
   of the room indicates all ones and twos, then the group can quickly see that
   consensus has been reached. If there are several people indicating threes and
   fours, or if there is even one five or six, further discussion will be needed to
   reach unity.
2. No matter what the poll indicates, it is a good idea to ask if there is need for
   further comments or discussion.
3. It is extremely important to remember that when even one person is not in unity
   with the decision, the group needs to take the time to hear and consider what
   the person has to say. Ask participants who have indicated that they do not
   agree with the decision and feel the need to stand in the way of this decision
   being accepted (five fingers), what would need to be changed for them to be
   comfortable joining the group in an agreement on the subject. See if there are
   changes in wording, further definitions, the addition of exceptions, or amend-
   ments that would make the option acceptable. If so, any change would need to
   be checked with the whole group.

Deciding → Consensus

Levels of Consensus, Continued

4. If that person is still not in consensus with the group, then the group needs to decide whether the decision making will be carried over to a later time to give more time for reflection, research, etc.; whether they will continue discussion until they are able to find an acceptable solution; or whether they will use their fall-back decision making method.

Example:

The planning group for Forests Unlimited has been working on a mission statement for two meetings. Participants seem close to agreeing on the statement, but several people haven't said much. You suggest checking on whether the group has reached agreement about the wording of the mission statement by using Levels of Consensus. After reminding the group of the process, you ask for a "show of fingers." In scanning the room, everyone can see that there are four people holding up one finger, five holding up two fingers, one person holding up three fingers, and one person holding up four fingers. You summarize what you see, and then ask Lena, who is holding up four fingers, to articulate her concern about the mission statement. Lena says, "I'm concerned we won't be able to live up to all that this mission statement implies." You ask the group for comments; they say that when it comes to the next stage of the process, setting goals, the group will focus on what is "doable" in the short term. Lena thanks them for the reminder, and puts up three fingers.

Levels of Consensus, Continued

The Levels of Consensus:

(1) I can say an unqualified "yes" to the decision. I am satisfied that the decision is an expression of the wisdom of the group.

(2) I find the decision perfectly acceptable.

(3) I can live with the decision; I'm not especially enthusiastic about it.

(4) I do not fully agree with the decision and need to register my view about why. However, I do not choose to block the decision. I am willing to support the decision because I trust the wisdom of the group.

(5) I do not agree with the decision and feel the need to stand in the way of this decision being accepted.

(6) I feel that we have no clear sense of unity in the group. We need to do more work before consensus can be reached.

Deciding → Consensus

Stoplight Cards

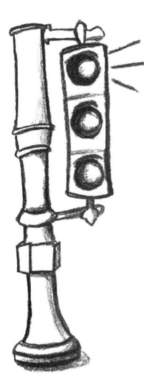

Stoplight cards is a decision making method, similar to Levels of Consensus, but uses red, yellow and green cards, rather than fingers, to indicate agreement, hesitation or disagreement with the decision being proposed.

When it is useful:

- when you don't need a very subtle understanding of people's positions
- when you need to be moving more quickly than Levels of Consensus allows
- when holding up fingers is uncomfortable for the group

How to use it:

1. Distribute red, green and yellow index cards or sheets of paper to each participant.
2. When a decision is being proposed, ask group members to indicate with the appropriate card how they feel about the decision:
   - Green means agreement with the decision.
   - Yellow means some hesitation or caution about the decision, or it can be defined as "I can live with it."
   - Red means disagreement or "no go" with the decision.
3. As with Levels of Consensus, any indication of hesitation or disagreement calls for further discussion.

Example:

First Congregational Church is hiring a new Regigious Education Coordinator. After much discussion, the committee has developed a tentative job description. You suggest checking for group agreement on the description by using Stoplight Cards. After reminding the group of the process, you ask for a "show of cards." Two people are holding up green; three are holding up yellow, and one is holding up red. You summarize what you see and then turn to the person with the red card. Marietta tells the group that she thinks the money should be spent on missions and that a volunteer should be found for this position; therefore she can't support this expenditure of church funds. After some discussion,

Stoplight Cards, Continued

the group decides to finalize the job desciption but put off advertising the position until they see if they can find a qualified volunteer. They agree that at the next meeting they will have to make a final decision. You then ask those with yellow cards what their hesitation is. They raise concerns about the language in the job description. After some talk, the group works out the wording and schedules their next meeting.

Deciding → Consensus

Thumbs Up

Thumbs up is a pared down version of the six finger method. It is simpler; the disadvantage is that you lose the gradations that Levels of Consensus offers.

When it is useful:

- when you don't need a very subtle understanding of people's positions
- when you need to be moving more quickly than Levels of Consensus allows

How to use it:

1. Develop a shared definition of what each thumb position means:
   - Thumb up means agreement with the decision.
   - Thumb straight across means some hesitation or caution about the decision, or it can mean neutrality such as, "I can live with it," or "I don't feel strongly one way or the other." Be sure to get agreement in the group as to the meaning of this signal.
   - Thumb down means disagreement or "no go" with the decision.
2. Ask group members to indicate with their thumbs how they feel about the proposed decision.
3. As with Levels of Consensus, indication of hesitation or disagreement calls for further discussion.

Example:

First Congregational Church is hiring a new Regigious Education Coordinator. After much discussion, the committee has developed a tentative job description. You suggest checking for group agreement on the description by using Thumbs Up. After reminding the group of the process, you ask for a "show of thumbs." Four people have their thumbs up and one is showing thumbs down. You summarize what you see and then turn to the person with her thumb down. Vivian tells the group that she thinks the money should be spent on missions and that a volunteer should be found for this position; therefore she can't support this expenditure of church funds. After some discussion, the group decides to finalize the job desciption but put off advertising the position until they see if they can find a qualified volunteer. They schedule a future meeting, at which time they agree to make a final decision.

Sense of the Group

Often in the process of a meeting, you, as facilitator, will have a sense of the direction of the group. You will have been listening intently to the opinions and concerns of the participants, paying attention to how many participants have spoken, watching all the other clues which tell you where the group's thinking is. You will often hear their areas of agreement before the participants do. Sense of the Group means reflecting back that understanding to the group and checking to see if you are correct.

When it is useful:

- when you are hearing areas of agreement in the group, which could help them come to a decision
- when the group seems confused or stuck and could be helped by hearing your reflections on areas of agreement or key themes and issues

How to use it:

1. Listen intently to each participant and to the direction of the group as a whole.
2. When enough people have spoken and you have heard areas of agreement or key themes emerging, share your sense of the group's direction with them.
3. Check with the group to see if that makes sense to them. Check carefully to make sure that you aren't leading the group somewhere that they don't want to go.
4. If the group is comfortable with your articulation of the sense of the group (or have amended it to suit their needs), then record the agreement.

Cautions:

You need to be very aware of your own opinions and biases and make sure that you are not suggesting your own thinking to the group rather than truly reflecting their thinking. It is important to use a tone of questioning and checking to see if you are on the right track.

Example:

Your group has been working on whether or not to expand the child care facilities to accommodate infants. There has been considerable comment from more than half the group about the need for infant services. There has been some resistance from those who are concerned that it would be a money losing venture and endanger the other services. Everyone agrees that there is a room avail-

Deciding → Sense of the Group

Sense of the Group, Continued

able, but it would cost money to make it suitable for infant care and no one is sure where the money would come from. It is your sense that everyone feels that the service is needed, that a room exists which could serve that purpose and that the slots would fill quickly. However, the group is unwilling to commit to the new service without knowing the financial needs and ramifications. You reflect back to the group. "It's my sense that most all of you agree that the service is needed, that it would fill rapidly and that the room could accommodate it. But, you need a more detailed analysis of the costs and financial viability of the service. Is that correct? Is anyone hearing it differently?" If the group agrees, then you can ask them what they want to do as a next step to get the information they need to make a decision.

Great Meetings!

great results

Chapter Seven:
Maximizing Your Group's Potential

EVERY GROUP HAS ENORMOUS POTENTIAL TO BE CREATIVE AND ACCOMPLISH GOOD work. Helping groups to maximize their potential is one of the purposes of facilitation. Some groups are like white water rapids, spilling over with exciting, somewhat chaotic energy and momentum. In such a group, your challenge as facilitator will be to provide processes to channel the group's energy to its best use. Other groups are like a still pond, quiet with little outward activity. For such a group, your work will be to get the waters stirred up a bit — using warm-up activities to generate energy and encouraging the participation needed for a group to identify important issues, clarify its goals, problem solve and make decisions. And still other groups are like a meandering river, winding here and there on its destination to the sea. Here your facilitation work will be to help keep the group on track so it doesn't use its energy in needless digressions.

In this chapter, we offer several suggestions for warm up activities, encouraging participation, keeping groups on track, and getting them back on track when needed. Some of the concepts in this chapter necessarily overlap with the previous chapter, *Chapter Six: Choosing the Right Tool.* There we describe in detail many different tools to fit various types and sizes of groups.

Encouraging Participation from Start to Finish

People participate in groups when they have something to say, trust that their input is taken seriously, feel safe in expressing their ideas and opinions and are given opportunities for participation. Simple as that is to say, every facilitator knows there are many factors that influence group participation. For a fuller discussion of group dynamics see *Chapter Two: Knowing Your Group.*

GUIDELINES FOR MAXIMIZING PARTICIPATION

1. Begin by being participative in your planning: build desired outcome statements and an agenda with your client or group prior to the meeting.

2. Make meetings belong to everyone by sharing jobs: have participants bring refreshments, set up the room, keep time, record information, etc.

3. Use techniques that encourage participation, e.g., paired brainstorming, Quaker dialogue. Give immediate positive feedback on participation. Acknowledge the value of all behaviors that serve the group, whether task or social behaviors.

4. Allow people time to think. Some people process information and questions more slowly than others. Where appropriate, ask people to write their ideas first and then discuss. See "Brainstorming and its Variations"on page 80 of *Chapter Six: Choosing the Right Tool.*

5. Intervene at the first sign of a personal attack so that participants know it is

safe to contribute ideas and opinions.

6. Before the next meeting, or at a break, talk to individuals who aren't participating, and invite their participation. Try to identify an area of expertise or
   special perspective they bring that is crucial to the group.

7. If the group has some participants who dominate, establish a ground rule
   that everyone speaks once before anyone speaks a second
   time, or some similar rule that enables equal participation.

8. Separate the generation of ideas from the assignment of
   responsibilities. Just because Latisha proposed a solution to
   the problem doesn't necessarily mean she should be the
   one to implement it.

> *Separate
> the generation
> of ideas from
> the assignment
> of responsibilities.*

9. If the group as a whole is silent and various techniques
   don't increase participation, ask the group for its understanding of why there is no participation. Is it time of day,
   lack of understanding, fear of having to do more work? If
   this question fails to get a response, there is a good chance that something
   (mistrust, anger, fear) is present to such a degree that no one will risk sharing in a group setting. One-on-one conversations might reveal the problem.

10. Remember that silence does not equal non-participation. A participant may
    be waiting to speak until she has a real contribution to make.

Warm-up Exercises

There are a variety of exercises that help group members to get to know one another, break the ice, restore energy after lunch or illustrate a point. On the following
pages we have described a few. The chapter on *Reading and Resources* also offers suggestions for additional reading that will provide you with even more warm-up exercises. Note: In all introduction exercises, it is important to structure the exercise so
that you respect the individual's right to control what and how much is disclosed.

Everyone Who Has Ever...

When it is useful:

- as an energizer
- as a way to help a group know more about its members
- in groups of 8-40

How to use it:

1. You will need a bean bag or other object which can serve as a base on the ground for each person in the group.
2. This exercise is a second cousin to the musical chairs game you played as a child. Assemble the group standing in a circle. Give each person a "base" to put on the ground by her spot. You stand in the middle of the circle without a base.
3. Explain that whoever is in the center needs to think of something interesting, mundane, unusual she may have done in her life. The person in the center gives the instruction: "Everyone who has ever milked a cow change places." Everyone who has milked a cow (and is willing to admit to it) must change to a different base while the person in the center is also trying to find a base. The result will be that someone different will be left without a base and will become the person in the center.
4. The process begins again. The person in the center can choose any activity as long as she has actually done it herself.
5. The game can go on until everyone has been trapped in the middle or until you run out of time.

Gallery Walk

When it is useful:

- in group forming
- in groups of 8-20

How to use it:

1. You will need a piece of flipchart paper for each participant and watercolor pens.
2. Ask the participants to draw an image or series of
   images that create a picture of who they are and what is most important to
   them. Reinforce that this is not an exercise about artistic talent, just an effort to
   use images to introduce themselves to one another. Do one for yourself quickly
   as an example showing trees and mountains for your interest in hiking, stick figures for the members of your family, books for your pleasure in reading novels
   and so on.
3. Give the group 5-10 minutes to work on their drawings. If you have the wall
   space to hang them up, ask the group to do so. Then walk around the gallery
   asking each person to introduce herself through his picture.

Getting Acquainted BINGO

When it is useful:

- in group forming
- as a way to learn group members' names
- as a way to help group members know more about its members
- in groups of 10 or more

How to use it:

1. Ahead of time prepare 3 different bingo cards, each with 5 spaces across and 5
   down. You can either title it BINGO, or use your organization's first letter to
   make it XINGO for (Xeno Corporation) or WINGO (for Welcome Club). On
   each of the spaces put a blank (for the name) and then a short statement. Be
   sure that the statement fits someone in the group and is appropriate for the
   nature of the group.

Sample statements:

_____has worked for Xeno Corporation for less than one year

_____has belonged to the Welcome Club for more than 5 years

_____has a dog

_____likes to ski

2. Ahead of time shuffle the three versions of the cards
3. Write the instructions on a flipchart: Introduce yourself to another group member and find out if any of the BINGO statements fits that person. If so, write that person's name in the space.
4. As people arrive, give each one a BINGO card and explain the rules. If the group is small, they can use any person's name in up to 3 spaces. If the group is large – 25 or more – they can use each person only one time
5. You can either have small prizes for people as they complete their cards, or encourage them to join someone who hasn't finished to help them get all their spaces filled.

B	I	N	G	O
Has run in a road race	Likes to snowboard	Has never tried sushi	Has performed on a stage	Went to summer camp
Has held public office	Went abroad in college	Has coached a sport	Loves cold weather	Balances checkbook to the penny
Still has a friend from junior high	Drives the same make of car as you	Has been to Niagara Falls	Plays chess	Plays the Lottery
Has at least two pets	Is afraid of heights	Is a vegetarian	Has flown in a helicopter	Has used a mitre saw

Name Juggle

When it is useful:

- early in group forming
- in groups of 6-25
- as an energizer after lunch
- to illustrate a point about how many balls everyone has in the air at once

How to use it:

1. You will need a collection of tennis balls, bean bags or stuffed animals (anything small and soft that you can throw around), preferably as many objects as you have people.

2. Assemble the group standing in a circle. If the participants are wearing name tags, have them put the tags on their backs or out of sight. Start with one of your throwable objects. Explain that participants are going to throw it around the group from one member to another until all participants have had a chance to catch and throw it once.

3. Each participant must call out the name of the person to whom they are going to throw the ball before they throw it. The receiver must then thank the thrower by name. Encourage the participants to remember from whom they received the ball and to whom they threw it, because they will need to repeat that sequence.

4. In the first round, it helps to ask each participant to raise her hand after she has caught and thrown the ball to indicate that she has already had a turn.

5. Try the first round. Make sure everyone has a turn, no one has it twice, everyone remembered to call out the name of the receiver and to thank the thrower by name.

6. Once the group has the system down, begin steadily introducing more balls into the system until the group has nearly as many objects in the air as there are people. It will be noisy and a little crazy, but if you set a tone of calm, steady attention the group will follow. Finally, you stop adding new objects and the last ones make their way around.

7. Take a moment to debrief the exercise, asking what the experience was like for the group.

Organize by Birthdays

When it is useful:

- as a team building activity
- as an energizer after lunch
- to help groups who are working on leadership or problem solving questions
- in groups of any size

How to use it:

1. Explain to the group that their assignment is to organize themselves by their birthdays. Give them no further instructions. You are intentionally giving them an ambiguous assignment. Birthday could be interpreted to mean year of birth, month or day of birth, or other variations. What you are actually asking them to do is to figure out how they want to define it and then implement that order.
2. Your job is to observe their process, looking for how leadership emerges, what roles different members of the group play, what processes they use, and so on. Debrief by asking them to reflect on their own process and, where helpful, sharing your observations.

Personal Attribute

When it is useful:

- to help a group get to know one another better
- as an energizer
- in groups of any size

How to use it:

1. You will need index cards or similar paper and a basket to collect the cards.
2. Ask everyone to write on the card something about themselves no one is likely to know. E.g. I'm a certified underwater diver. I grew up in Africa. I write poetry, etc.
3. Then collect the cards in a basket.
4. Each participant draws a card from the basket and has to locate the person who wrote the card. (If the person draws her own card, she needs to draw another.)
5. Participants sit down when they have identified the writer of the card they chose and have also been found.
6. After everyone is sitting, go around and read the information from the cards.

Something in Common

When it is useful:

- early in group forming
- in groups where people know each other superficially
- when two groups or organizations are merging
- in groups with strong differences or conflicts

How to use it:

1. Ask the group to break into pairs. Give the pairs 1-2 minutes to find something that they have in common which is not obvious. That they both wear glasses, have black hair or are women doesn't count; it must be something which requires discussion to find out. At the end of the time, sample a few of the results.
2. Then ask the pairs to join up with another pair to make a group of four. Give the groups 2-4 minutes to find something that all four have in common that was not mentioned in the first round. Again, sample a few of the results.
3. If your group is large enough and you have time, try again in groups of eight, or the entire group.

Something in Your Pocket

When it is useful:

- in group forming
- as a quick get-to-know you exercise

How to use it:

1. Ask people to find something they have with them (e.g., jewelry, something they are wearing, an item in their wallet or pocketbook) that tells something about them that others didn't know.
2. Introduce yourself first to model how you want introductions to go. You might say " I always carry this little multitool because I'm a fix-it type of person" or "I wear this amethyst ring because it reminds me of the wonderful vacation with special friends."
3. Ask each person to introduce themselves and their item. (If they don't have anything with them, it's fine for them to describe whatever they want.)

Demonstating Our Diversity

When it is useful:

- to help members of a group learn more about one another
- to understand some of the diversity within the group
- as an energizer

How to use it:

1. Ask the group to sort itself based on characteristics you pose to them. For example: "Everyone who grew up in Maine go to this corner of the room and everyone who has moved here as an adult go to that corner. Or "everyone who worked for the company before 2000 stand up and everyone who has joined the company since then stay seated."
2. If it is appropriate, ask how this diversity impacts the group.
3. Choose elements of diversity which support or impact your group's work. Avoid controversial or topical divisions (such as politics and religion), since the purpose of the exercise is to appreciate differences and gain a greater appreciation of one another, not to become polarized.

Three Balls

When it is useful:

- as an energizer after lunch
- in a group that is working on problem solving
- in a group where you want to emphasize thinking outside of the box
- in groups of 8-20

How to use it:

1. You will need three balls or bean bags and a watch with a second hand.
2. Assemble the group standing in a circle. Explain that you are going to throw a ball or bean bag to a participant, who will then throw it on to another, until everyone in the group has had a turn. It helps if the participants raise their hands

after they have had a turn so that the others can see who hasn't had a turn.

3. Remind the group that they are to be gentle in throwing and that they need to remember their sequence, since you will ask them to repeat that sequence each time they throw the ball around the group. Start the first round to get the sequence established.

4. Now tell them that you are going to add two more balls after the first one and these must also be passed around the same sequence. Give it a trial run with the three balls, starting one after the other.

5. Now tell the group that you are going to time them to see how quickly they can accomplish the task. Remind them that everyone must handle each ball and that it must go in the established sequence. Start counting the time when you throw the first ball and stop when all three are back to you again. Tell them how long it took.

6. Ask if the group can cut the time in half. Start the process again. The group may ask you if they can move closer together or change places. The only rules that you have for them is that everyone must handle each ball and that it must go in the established sequence. If they need time to talk among themselves that is fine. Eventually they will be ready to try again. Time them again.

7. Now ask them if they can cut the time in half again. This will definitely generate some group discussion. They may choose some significant restructuring of how they are doing it. Everything is acceptable as long as everyone handles each ball and it goes in the established sequence.

8. Finally they will be down to a few seconds and you can call it off. Ask the group what its presumptions were about the "rules" in the beginning and what it took to reduce the times. It requires letting go of assumptions about the order they stand in, where they stand, what "touching" or "handling" the ball means.

Three Questions in Pairs

When it is useful:

- in group forming
- as an energizer
- in any size group

How to use it:

1. Ask the group members to stand up and find a partner. If you have an uneven number there will be a trio.

2. Next, explain that each pair has one minute to tell one another every living thing in their households from significant other, to plants and mold in the refrigerator. Keep it light and brief.

3. When the minute is up, ask them to change partners. This time ask them a question which is somewhat related to their work at hand and give them 2-4 minutes. For example, if they are nervous about the planning process they're working on ask them, "What is the most exciting, positive possibility that you think the future holds for the organization?" They then have 1-2 minutes each to tell their partner their idea. Remember that this is just a short warm up exercise so be sure to ask questions that can be answered quickly.

4. Ask the group to change partners again and ask them another question with some relevance to their work, again giving them 2-4 minutes. After you have finished, ask the groups to briefly report some of the ideas.

Three Truths and a Lie

When it is useful:

- in group forming when group members are ready to learn a little more about one another
- as an energizer
- in groups of 8-20

How to use it:

1. You will need index cards and pins.

2. Give each participant an index card or 3x5 piece of paper. Ask each person to write four things about themselves on the card in print large enough for others to read easily. Three of the things should be true; one should be false. Ask them to pin the card on like a name tag.

3. Now ask the group to circulate, pairing up with people to try to guess which item on the other person's list is not true. Ask them to continue circulating until they have seen every member of the group. Remember with an uneven number of people there will always be a trio.

Methods for Generating Discussion

Discussion is the backbone of any meeting, yet groups often have difficulty opening up. Depending on the size and type of the group, the time of day and the stage of group development, different methods of generating discussion will be appropriate. It's good to have a spare method or two in your hip pocket in case the one you have chosen first doesn't invoke the depth of discussion needed.

Discussion by Categories of Participants

How to use it:

If there is a reason to do so, call on people by categories, e.g. employees with more/less than five years with the company; supervisors or team leaders; union/non-union; men/women to discuss the issue at hand. Sometimes it helps these categories of participants to think through their perspective.

Pros and Cons:

- It may draw out particular perspectives that would otherwise not have emerged.
- If there are different power levels present, it may encourage those who perceive themselves to have less power to speak out.
- It can create or reinforce divisions.
- People can feel put on the spot.

Pre-Discussion Quiet Time

How to use it:

Give participants a few minutes to write down some thoughts about the topic, and then ask for their contributions.

Pros and Cons:

- It gives each person thinking time, which is especially appreciated by introverts.
- It can make for more balanced participation and a more thoughtful discussion.
- Some people may be uncomfortable with silence.
- It may quiet the energy of the group.

Quaker Dialogue

How to use it:

Named for the Quaker tradition of silence and listening, Quaker Dialogue is a discussion method that promotes equal participation and careful listening. This method of discussion is useful when equality of participation is important or when group members need to listen to one another attentively.

1. Explain the process and rules for Quaker Dialogue: Anyone is free to pass; and no one comments on another's contribution until everyone has had a chance to speak. It might be a good idea to put a time limit on each person's speaking, if necessary.
2. Go around the room offering each person the opportunity to give her thoughts on a subject without being interrupted or questioned.
3. Before opening the floor to questions and discussion, check with the people who passed during the first round to see if they want to speak.

Pros and Cons:

- Each person is given an equal voice.
- When the members of the group don't seem to be listening to one another, this method encourages better listening.
- When individuals aren't participating, this gives them a way to get involved.
- A sense of the group often evolves from the collective comments of individuals.
- The process can get bogged down, especially with a large group, and drain energy.
- Some people are uncomfortable being in the spotlight.

Small Group Discussion

How to use it:

The whole group is divided into sub-groups. Each small group can address the same question or be given different questions. If the small group is expected to report back to the full group, make sure a recorder and reporter are selected at the beginning of the discussion. Each group can take turns relaying the key points of its discussion.

Remember: the smaller the group the higher the percentage of participation you can expect. For example, in a two person group, 100% participation is almost guaranteed. In a five person group, participation may be considerably less.

Pros and Cons:

- Usually the comfort level is higher in a small group, which leads to greater participation.
- This method gives everyone the opportunity to speak.
- The sound of people speaking in the room can energize everyone.
- The facilitator or leader can't be sure that the groups are on track.
- Self-oriented behaviors such as dominating or complaining can negatively affect the sub-group and are harder to confront in a small group.
- Groups complete their tasks at different rates.
- Reporting back can be tedious. To increase attentiveness, encourage reporters to give the highlights of the sub-group's discussion, not to read back everything the group developed.

Whole Group Discussion

How to use it:

The group is asked a question or given a problem to which anyone may respond. Generally it works better to ask an open-ended question (e.g., how could this problem be solved?), that invites a longer response rather than closed-ended questions (e.g., is this problem solvable?), that only require a yes or no answer.

Pros and Cons:

- When the members of a group are engaged in the topic, this method of discussion is lively. Energy is created and a good product can result.
- The smaller the group, the more likely that everyone who wants to will participate.
- If members of the group don't participate voluntarily, or if some members dominate while others are silent, the energy of the group can be sapped.
- Because of time limitations, everyone may not have the opportunity to speak.

Keeping Groups on Track

> Being on track means the group is progressing toward its agreed-upon goal; it doesn't mean that every minute has to be regimented.

Being on track in a group means that the group is progressing toward its agreed-upon goal. This doesn't mean that every minute of the meeting has to be regimented; there should be enough latitude for creative brainstorms and humor as well as the group's social needs.

There are several steps a group can take to ensure they are in agreement about the direction of their meeting:

1. Establish and get agreement on a clear agenda that has realistic time limits. Put the agenda on a flipchart or white board where everyone can see it.

2. Establish ground rules about discussions that aren't relevan to the agenda, additional agenda items that may crop up during the meeting and anything else that might take the group away from its task. Use the parking lot to capture these ideas. For more information on the concept of the parking lot, refer to page 46 of *Chapter Four: Designing a Great Meeting*.

3. Establish roles such as time keeper, break monitor, etc.

WHEN THE GROUP IS OFF TRACK

The first step to helping a group get back on track is to analyze why they have gone off track in the first place. The following questions investigate the major reasons groups get off track.

1. Is the goal of the meeting clear? "If you don't know where you are going you're liable to end up somewhere else." — Robert Mager

2. Are the steps to reaching that goal clear? For example, do all group members understand the process steps? See *Chapter Five: Understanding Process* for details.

3. Is the group finding it difficult to start discussion about a particular issue?

4. Are there issues about trust of the leader or individuals within the group?

5. Are individuals attending to their own needs over the group needs: telling stories, suggesting new agenda items, rather than focusing on accomplishing the task?

GETTING BACK ON TRACK

Obviously, how you get the group back on track will depend on your analysis of the situation. Here are some suggestions:

1. Physically point out on the flipchart where the group is in terms of the agenda. Remind the group why it needs to be where it is. For example: "George, it sounds as if you 're ready to make a decision, but the group has agreed to spend thirty minutes generating options. Please hold your solution until we get to that on the agenda; then we can take the time to hear your thinking in more detail." Such an intervention affirms the participant and also puts the group back to the appropriate place on the agenda.

2. If someone seems to be wandering off track, ask the person to relate her point to the topic at hand. For example, "Harriet, I'm not sure I see the connection between last year's sales goals and the company's environmental policies (the topic of the meeting). Could you explain the linkage for us?"

3. Ask the group if a particular diversion is helpful in moving toward its goal. For example: "We didn't make time on the agenda to talk about the impact of a good environmental policy on company profitability; do you think it would be helpful to talk about that now? If so, what section of the agenda shall we take the time from?"

4. Name what you are perceiving. For example: "We've been trying to start this discussion for ten minutes without much progress. I get a sense that people are reluctant to talk about a downsizing policy. Am I right?" Or, more generally: "It seems like we're having a tough time sticking to the agenda. What's going on?"

Great Meetings!

great results

Chapter Eight
Promoting Positive Communication

EVERYTHING THAT GOES ON IN A MEETING INVOLVES COMMUNICATION: LISTENING, expressing opinions, reporting information, questioning and decision making. The facilitator is the group's model, teacher and monitor of quality communication. It's easy to see then that communication is the bedrock skill for an effective facilitator.

Setting the Tone

First, a facilitator needs to create an atmosphere in which good communication can happen. Here are some ways to set the appropriate tone.

HAVE THE ROOM READY: Having the room prepared gives the message that you know what you are doing and are taking the meeting seriously. Make sure the room is ready to go when participants arrive, or enlist the help of early arrivals. Include the following items:

- flipchart paper and markers
- chairs and/or tables arranged to encourage collaboration
- name tags or name tents ready to be filled in
- prepared flipcharts, audio-visual equipment, handouts, etc.

For more information on room setups, see *Chapter Four: Designing a Great Meeting*.

BE THERE TO GREET MEETING MEMBERS: When appropriate, make a personal connection with each person. This connection will give you information about who the participants are and will give them a chance to get to know you.

CREATE AND BE SENSITIVE TO THE TONE OF THE MEETING: Create a positive tone for the group at every opportunity: be sincere, upbeat and human. Pay attention to the mood of people as they arrive; you're likely to get helpful information regarding the attitudes of group members. For example, if you hear lots of grumbling about having to attend this meeting or mumbling about a waste of time, you will want to address that issue when the whole group is assembled. Say something like, "I heard some comments as you all were coming in that made me think that the time spent here needs to be very productive. How can we make sure that happens?" If people are arriving in a jovial mood, don't be too serious or formal. Conversely, if people are very tense and quiet, don't be flip. Your behavior will convey the message that you are paying attention to the nature of the group. Even if you are working with a regularly scheduled group, where everyone is quite familiar with one another, don't overlook the importance of setting a helpful tone.

Listening Skills

Excellent listening skills are fundamental to good facilitation. There are two types of listening — non-verbal and verbal. Non-verbal listening involves using eye contact, body position, encouraging expressions and silence to convey your attentiveness and interest in what a person is saying. Verbal, or reflective, listening refers to the service you provide in reflecting back what the speaker has said and clarifying your understanding of what he meant. Most often you will use and encourage both ways of listening. It's important to remember that listening does not involve agreeing or disagreeing, giving your opinion (either verbally or non-verbally) or adding your story.

> **Note:**
>
> We have moved away from the once-common terminology of "active" and "passive" listening, because our experience is that all facilitative listening requires active engagement.

Non-verbal Listening Skills

As implied by the title, non-verbal listening means the listener is not speaking back to the talker. Some of the components of a facilitator's non-verbal listening are:

GOOD EYE CONTACT: Generally speaking, maintain eye contact 70-80% of the time. However, it's important to remember that different cultures have different customs about eye contact. In some cultures, direct prolonged eye contact is considered disrespectful. Be sensitive to whom you are listening.

BODY POSITIONING: If you have been standing, sitting on the edge of a table or in a chair will convey a sense of equality. A relaxed posture is usually most effective.

FACIAL EXPRESSIONS: Nodding and facial expressions have great impact on the person who is speaking. If you are uncertain about the impact of your facial expression, or receive feedback that you look irritated, bored, happy, etc. when you are not meaning to convey those feelings, you may want to watch yourself on videotape or practice in front of a mirror. That way you can be sure that your intent is mirrored on your face.

ENCOURAGING EXPRESSIONS: These run the gamut from door openers such as, "Say more about that," "I'd like to hear," to encouraging grunts such as: Oh, Hmmm, Really, Ah...of course, and so forth. These are to let the person know you are listening without breaking the flow of conversation.

SILENCE: Silence is an important component of facilitation. People often need time to frame what they want to say before speaking. A comfortable silence will often encourage the speaker to talk. As a facilitator, value silence.

Verbal (Reflective) Listening Skills

Being a mirror is an important skill for the facilitator. Reflective listening is the process of reflecting back what an individual or the group has said in order to confirm your understanding and to allow them to hear what they have said.

Depending on the situation, you may choose to reflect back the literal content of the message, your perception of the meaning behind the content and/or the feeling expressed behind the content. Or you may need to ask a question for clarification.

For example, Hallie says, "I'm tired of this whole process." You might reflect that back in several ways:

Literal Content: "Hallie, so you are tired of the whole planning process."

Underlying Meaning: "Hallie, it sounds as if you would like to make a change in how we are proceeding."

Underlying Feelings: "Hallie, you sound frustrated with the way this decision making process is going."

Ask a Question: "Hallie, tell me more about why you are tired of the process."

Listening is a very powerful tool. A good listener can help the speaker gain greater understanding of himself and even assist the individual or group in problem solving.

Hints for Reflective Listening

FEELINGS: Try to identify the feeling without either overstating or understating it. Don't worry too much, though, because if you miscalculate the intensity of the feeling, the speaker will almost always correct you. Remember to keep your own feelings out of your statement.

SUMMARIZE: At the end of a lengthy explanation or discourse, it is often helpful for the facilitator to "sum up" the gist of what the speaker has just said. Doing this helps everyone focus on what has just been said and promotes clear communication.

"You" and "I" Messages

"You" messages
label the receiver
rather than describe
the speaker's needs

"You" statements often leave the receiver of the message feeling threatened and defensive. This type of message can increase tension. "You" messages remove the ownership for behavior from the person speaking and label the receiver instead of describing the thoughts, needs or feelings of the speaker. Common "you" messages include the following:

- Orders and commands: "Stop doing that!" " Get on with the agenda."
- Blaming and name-calling: "You are always late and disrupt everyone!" "You're driving me crazy!"
- Threats: "If you continue pushing this idea, you will force me to withdraw from the committee."
- Statements that give solutions but do not explain them: "You should forget about that idea."

"I" messages
promote positive
communication and
foster effective
interpersonal
relationships

"I" messages promote positive communication, which in turn fosters effective interpersonal relationships. They promote ownership by the speaker of his needs, wants, and feelings, rather than a projection onto the listener. As a facilitator, you want to steer people away from "you" messages and toward "I" messages modeling "I" messages whenever possible. Below are some examples of "I" messages:

- "I need a stretch break right now," rather than, "Anybody need a break?"
- "I'm frustrated by the lack of information," rather than, "Your committee did a lousy job of collecting information."
- "I am furious that the council didn't fund this project," rather than, "You all deserve to be recalled."

If you, as facilitator, are not hearing "I" messages, you can restate what is said or ask a question. For example, if someone says, "Your committee did a lousy job of collecting information," you might restate it: "Paolo, you're pretty frustrated at not having the information the group needs here." Then remind people that it's helpful to the group to use "I" messages.

"I" Messages are Effective Because They:

- place responsibility with the sender of the message.
- reduce the other person's defensiveness and resistance to further communication.
- provide information about the impact of the other person's behavior without evaluating it.
- promote open, adult-to-adult communication.
- build trust, create empathy, and facilitate understanding between sender and receiver and the whole group.

The Art of Effective Questioning

Asking questions so that you get useful, constructive answers is an art that is mastered through experience. It's important to know your own assumptions, values, and biases, so that they don't become obstacles to effective questioning, either through the words you choose or as reflected in tone or body language. In this section, we will consider four types of useful questions, and one type to avoid.

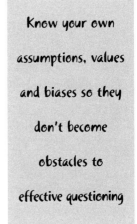

Know your own assumptions, values and biases so they don't become obstacles to effective questioning

<u>DIRECT QUESTIONS</u>: Direct questions seek specific information. For example:

- "When did the budget shortfall become evident?"
- "Which three natural habitats are you referring to?"

If overused, however, direct questions may make individuals or groups feel they are being interrogated. Also, closed-ended questions, requiring only a yes or no answer, tend to shut down a discussion.

<u>OPEN-ENDED QUESTIONS</u>: Open-ended questions stimulate discussion and give more information about the issues to be addressed. For example:

- "What are the problems that concern you?"
- "What is the background to this situation?"
- "You referred to an incident in the park. Could you say more about that?"
- "Why does this solution appeal to you?"

<u>CLARIFYING QUESTIONS</u>: Clarifying questions clarify the listener's or speaker's perceptions:

- "I'm not sure I'm with you; do you mean....?"
- "Let me see if I understand you, you...?"
- "What's the difference between what's happening now and what you'd like to see happening...?"
- "First I heard you say you supported the idea; now I think you're saying you don't. Can you clarify your position for me?"

<u>PEEL THE ONION QUESTIONS</u>: Peel the onion questions facilitate a deeper understanding of the feelings involved in a situation or discussion. The turning point in a tough discussion often comes when the parties start to tell each other how they feel. For example:

- "You say you're worried that a pre-release residence might be located in your neighborhood. Can you say more about that?

Caution: Leading Questions!

Leading questions attempt to align the speaker with the questioner, by using such phrases as:

- "Don't you think....?"
- "Wouldn't you rather ....?"
- "You don't really think that's going to work...?"

Such questions should be phrased more directly. For example:

- "I think ending the meeting is a good idea. Do you agree?"
- "I think ending the meeting is a good idea. I hope you agree."
- "I'd like to end the meeting now. Is that okay with you?"

Reframing Language

In an attempt to encourage participants to understand one another's points of view, facilitators can help by restating judgmental or blaming language used by participants into more neutral language. By reframing the problem to focus on the issues and removing judgmental statements, you can enhance the ability of group members to hear each other. For example:

By reframing the problem, you can enhance the ability of group members to hear each other

GROUP MEMBER: "I put in hours of extra time doing what should have been Melissa's work. I can't believe she couldn't even show me the courtesy of a simple thank you."

FACILITATOR: "It sounds as if you worked hard to help Melissa out and are upset about her apparent lack of appreciation. What would be helpful for you now?"

Refocusing language is also appropriate when someone asks you a question that implies agreement. For example:

GROUP MEMBER: "Wouldn't you be mad if somebody said they were coming prepared to the meeting and then didn't?"

FACILITATOR: "Since I'm facilitating, I'll leave my opinion out of it. However, it seems as if it's creating a problem for you that those materials aren't here."

Great Meetings!

great results

Chapter Nine
Managing Conflict in Groups

CONFLICT IS A NORMAL, NATURAL PART OF HUMAN INTERACTION AND SOONER OR LATER it is part of virtually every group's experience. It is important to recognize that conflict has the potential to be very healthy for the group. Conflict, when acknowledged and dealt with in a positive manner, can clarify differences, increase the creativity of the group and build a strong team. On the other hand, if left untended, it can be damaging to the productivity and coherence of the group.

We define conflict as a problem that evokes strong feelings. A problem is a puzzle to be solved; a conflict is characterized by anger, frustration, sadness, etc. Understanding conflict and guiding a group in addressing conflict — rather than eliminating it — should be your goal as facilitator. Here are a few thoughts on conflict to keep in mind as we talk about managing conflict in groups.

Preventing Unnecessary Conflicts

First things first: many of the conflicts that arise in meetings can be prevented. As facilitator, you want to save people's energy for necessary conflicts by being skillful in preventing the unnecessary ones. Unnecessary conflicts are those conflicts that only serve to use up the time and energy of the group without producing a positive result. Examples of unnecessary conflicts are:

- Someone not bringing pertinent materials to a meeting. A phone call or e-mail asking that person to remember the materials would have prevented an unnecessary waste of people's time.
- An enthusiastic individual dominating the conversation because a ground rule was not established about equal participation.
- Group members being unsure what the role of their supervisor will be in the final decision making. A discussion at the start of the meeting about the extent of the group's decision making authority would clarify this.

Generally speaking, you can prevent such conflicts by doing a thorough job of assessment and preparation, and working with the group to be very clear about roles, responsibilities, ground rules, expected outcomes and decision making methods. The material in *Chapter Three: Getting a Good Start* and *Chapter Four: Designing a Great Meeting* provides detailed advice about preventing unnecessary conflicts.

Look for unexpected reactions to what you think is a completed discussion.

How do you tell the difference between an unnecessary and a necessary conflict? If you have identified a conflict as being one that can be prevented and yet the group continues to give evidence of a conflict, you may need to help the group deal with a deeper issue. Look for unexpected reactions to what you think is a completed discussion.

For example, you and the group spend time discussing who has the final decision making authority in the group. The supervisor, Amanda, says, "I will go along with whatever the group decides about a vacation policy." You paraphrase, "so whatever the group thinks will work the best, Amanda agrees to implement." As you say that, you see one person rolling his eyes and another pulling her chair back from the table and looking out the window. Oops, looks like the group has just hit an iceberg! At this point a skillful facilitator would assess that there is some issue here to be probed, a necessary conflict to be addressed, possibly about the trustworthiness of Amanda's promise.

Sources of Conflict

Often, we jump the gun by trying to solve a conflict before we have identified its roots. In order to deal with it satisfactorily, it's important to understand what caused it in the first place.

Knowing the sources of a conflict will help you, as facilitator, name the conflict for the group and choose a strategy for working with that conflict. There is great power in saying to a group, "I am hearing that you have very different priorities for how to spend this money," or "You are naming different needs that have brought you to serve on this board."

Most complex conflicts have their sources in several or all of the following categories:

MISCOMMUNICATION/MISINFORMATION: Miscommunication includes such dynamics as lack of information, inaccurate or assumed information, misunderstood information, inaccurate encoding or decoding of communication, and differing analyses of information. Examples of statements that would indicate miscommunication:

- "I never received that memo." (lack of communication or withholding of information)
- "I thought the CEO's announcement meant that everyone in Public Relations was getting laid off." (misinterpretation of data)

REAL OR PERCEIVED DIFFERENCES IN NEEDS AND PRIORITIES: Here we are referring to tangible needs such as competing demands for fiscal, material or time resources, as well as different priorities and methods for accomplishing tasks. This category also includes psychological needs, such as the need for security, competence, social acceptance or creativity. Examples of differences in needs:

- "I know he is very good at his job but I have three children to support." (conflicting needs for competence and security)
- The Director of Elderly Services says she needs 60% of the budgeted monies, but the Children's program needs 75% and it should be first priority. (competing fiscal needs)

REAL OR PERCEIVED DIFFERENCES IN VALUES, PERCEPTIONS, BELIEFS, ATTITUDES AND CULTURE: This is a broad and extremely important category that includes the totality of culture, personality, belief systems, etc. that form the lens through which we perceive and make meaning of the world. Examples of such differences:

- "He ought to know better than to speak to me like that." (differing social norms)
- "People who don't show up to work on time clearly don't care about their jobs." (perceived difference in work values)

STRUCTURAL CONDITIONS: Here we refer to situations where structures, whether physical, organizational or legal, are at the root of the conflict. Examples are lack of a clear task definition; unclear or missing descriptions of the role of members; physical distance between parts of organization; or regulations (terms of a labor management contract, ordinances, etc.). Statements that would indicate structural conflicts:

- "Working with staff on two different campuses is very difficult. (physical distance)
- "I did my best, but was never clear what my role was in this project." (lack of role clarity)

Hints on Identifying a Values Conflict

The words "should" or "ought to" will give you a clue to a values conflict. For example, if someone says, "He ought to know not to be late for this meeting," the speaker is describing her value system about lateness.

The greatest "heat" comes from values conflicts, because most people experience the clash of values and perceptions viscerally, as personal attacks rather than as interesting differences.

Intervening in Group Conflicts

To respond to conflict effectively, facilitators need a variety of skills and strategies, many of which are described below. Refer also to *Chapter Eight: Promoting Positive Communication*, and *Chapter Ten: Interventions: When to Step In*.

In every group it is important to acknowledge the value of conflict. Discuss with your group the fact that conflict can be valuable as a way to clarify points of view and to develop more creative products or services. You also want to affirm the value of — and right to — different opinions. It is natural that there are different opinions in a group.

Conflict can be valuable as a way to clarify points of view.

When there is conflict in a group, it is important to be aware of it and then assess what steps to take. The following intervention process can be used, whether the conflict is within the entire group, among two or more members, or between you and group members. Note: This process is similar to the one described in *Chapter Ten: Interventions: When to Step In*.

STEP I: READ THE GROUP: Conflict may be indicated by lack of eye contact, distancing body language, leaden silence, a shift in behavior from actively participating to withdrawing, attacks, tension, not listening, sarcasm or accusations.

STEP II: DECIDE WHETHER THE CONFLICT IS IMPACTING THE GROUP: Decide whether the conflict is impacting the group: There may be a minor disagreement between two people that has surfaced but doesn't affect the group's performance. While you may decide to let this type of conflict go, generally speaking, conflicts should be identified and addressed.

STEP III: NAME IT: Mirror what you see for the group, being careful not to blame the group. For example, "The group was having a lively discussion until Alicia made the comment about the budget. Then everyone got quiet. I wonder if there is some concern about the information Alicia gave?"

STEP IV: CHECK YOUR PERCEPTION WITH THE GROUP: Ask the group, "Do I have it right?"

STEP V: MAKE OR ASK FOR RECOMMENDATIONS TO ADDRESS THE SITUATION: What you do will depend on the type of conflict. Here are some possible interventions:

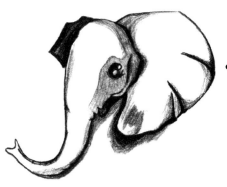

- Acknowledge the value of conflict. Discuss the value of conflict as a way to clarify points of view and to develop more creative products/services and stronger organizations.

- Name the source of the conflict as you see it: miscommunication, differences in needs or priorities, difference in values or beliefs and or structural conflict. Often it is an "elephant in the living room" that no one has dared acknowledge.

- Focus on outcomes and behavior, not values. In the case of a values conflict, help the group focus on the actual behavior or result they want, rather than on trying to change the conflicting values. While some might think everyone "should" dedicate their lives to the organization's fund raiser, the desired outcomes might be that the work gets done, that the needed money is raised and no one feels burned out afterwards.

- Use your ground rules. Refer to any ground rules that are relevant to the conflict. Examples of ground rules that support healthy conflict management include: one person speak at a time; attack the problem, not the person; people are encouraged to speak candidly; use "I messages" when giving opinions, listen with the goal of understanding the speaker.

- Look for common ground. Help the group discover where it does share common ground as well as where there are differences. Examples of common ground: joint desire for a good working relationship; importance of the company turning a profit; serving customers; protecting children, etc.

- Affirm the value of and right to different opinions. Discuss that different opinions are natural in a group. Make sure the group separates the difference of opinions from personal attacks on the person holding the opinions.

- Name the area of disagreement precisely. Make sure you are focusing on the right problem or conflict. You may be surprised how many problems go away simply by a more careful definition. For example, instead of, "John and Lea, you seem to disagree about flextime," say "John and Lea, you seem to disagree about whether flextime is possible in the personnel department during first shift."

- Grab hold of an agreement and build on it. Listen for areas where people agree or suggest common ground and point it out to the group. For example, "I heard both

> Listen for areas of common ground and point them out to the group.

Maria and Jeff say they were ready to work with the finance team. Who else is willing to do that?"

- Use the Aikido principle of moving with, rather than against, energy. Notice where an individual's energy or the group's energy is flowing and then move with it, rather than resist it. Reflective listening is one powerful way to do this.

- Take a break. When deadlocked, sometimes groups will benefit from a short change of scenery or a stretch. The mood can change dramatically after a break.

- Negotiate or mediate. Use the collaborative process described below as a guide when there is conflict between group members or between you and a group member.

Using the Collaborative Conflict Resolution Process in Groups

The collaborative conflict resolution process involves these steps:

ADDRESSING CONFLICT: Determining whether to address the conflict in a group setting or privately with the individuals involved requires some analysis.

- Does the problem belong to the whole group? If so, address it with everyone.
- Is the problem affecting the whole group? If so, name the problem to the group and ask the individuals involved whether they wish to address the conflict here or by themselves.

NAMING THE CONFLICT: If it is appropriate, name the conflict as you see it in tentative terms. For example, "Jake and Kara, you seem to have different views on this subject. I think it might be useful to take time to understand those different opinions." Or if the whole group is involved in expressing different opinions, you might say, "Everyone seems to have some strong opinions about flextime. Let's take time to make sure everyone has a chance to speak."

NEGOTIATING THE CONFLICT: If you need to guide two or more people through a negotiation process, use the following steps:

1. Explain to the group the process you'll be going through. You might even write the steps on a flipchart or easel.

2. Establish or reiterate the group's ground rules about each person having the opportunity to speak without interruption and making no personal attacks (i.e. focus on the problem, not the person).

3. Ask one person at a time to explain her view. "Joan, why don't you tell us your views about flextime." After she finishes, "Lily, tell us your viewpoint."

4. Summarize, or ask the group to summarize, each person's major points. If appropriate, ask the group to add additional views.

5. After every party to the conflict has spoken, summarize the issues that exist, "After listening to everyone speak, I hear the issues as being that flextime should be fair to each person, that it should not interfere with serving our customers, and that we need to rotate coverage. Did anyone hear any other issues?" Of course, you can also ask the group to summarize the issues for you.

6. If appropriate, take one issue at a time and work with it until you have a group agreement. Then take up the other issues, one at a time, until all have been discussed. An often-successful tactic is to start with the issue that will be easiest to resolve, so the group can get a sense of its ability to resolve an issue. Then the group can build on its success.

    > *Start with the issue that will be easiest to resolve so the group can build on its success.*

7. Summarize whatever agreement the group has made regarding the issues, including follow-up.

8. Mirror back to the group the good work it has just done.

In their book, <u>Getting to Yes: Negotiating Agreement without Giving in</u> (Houghton Mifflin Co, Boston, 1981), Roger Fisher and William Ury offer a four-step model for working out differences:

1. Separate the people from the problem: encourage careful listening and don't allow personal attacks.
2. Focus on interests, not positions: when someone states a position, ask "why" to learn about their underlying interests .
3. Invent options for mutual gain: use brainstorming to generate multiple options that meet everyone's interests.
4. Insist on objective criteria: ahead of time, establish criteria that will be mutually acceptable.

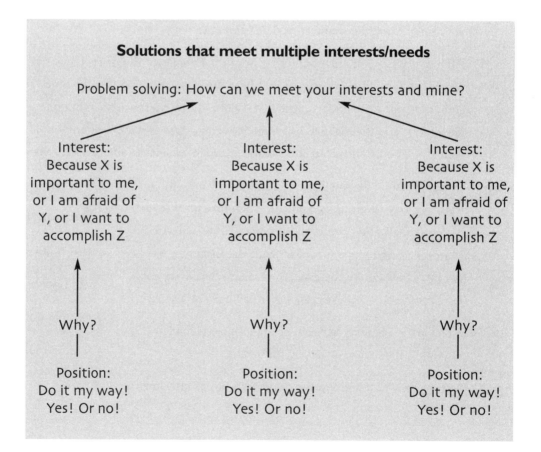

Solutions that meet multiple interests/needs

Problem solving: How can we meet your interests and mine?

| Interest: Because X is important to me, or I am afraid of Y, or I want to accomplish Z | Interest: Because X is important to me, or I am afraid of Y, or I want to accomplish Z | Interest: Because X is important to me, or I am afraid of Y, or I want to accomplish Z |

Why?   Why?   Why?

Position: Do it my way! Yes! Or no!   Position: Do it my way! Yes! Or no!   Position: Do it my way! Yes! Or no!

Structured Sharing of Conflicting Opinions

Encouraging open discussion is a tool for building understanding and reducing the heightened emotions around differing opinions which often block listening. One of the challenges when there is a conflict is how to move from a "crossed-arm" position to open discussion. Following is an easy-to-use method when there is a difference of opinion between two people, adapted from training work done by the National Coalition Building Institute.

The Process for Building Understanding Between Two People

STEP I: Person A states her opinion without interruption.

STEP II: Person B restates what he has heard person A say, without adding anything.

STEP III: B asks A questions to encourage her to explain why she has that particular opinion.

STEP IV: Switch roles. B states his opinion without interruption.

STEP V: A restates what she has heard person B say, without adding anything.

STEP VI: A asks B questions to encourage him to explain why he has that particular opinion.

STEP VII: Begin interactive discussion around the topic.

Note: Prior to the discussion, you may want to establish ground rules such as: let one person finish before another starts talking; no side conversations, etc.

Addressing Personal Conflicts in a Group Setting

Even conflict between two people can substantially disrupt a meeting. When you believe such a conflict is disruptive, it is important to address it. If the conflict seems to be just between two people, you might suggest the above process or ask if others in the group have concerns about the same topic. If you or the people involved don't feel it is appropriate to air their differences in front of the group, you might suggest that they agree to discuss it with each other before the next meeting and in the meantime agree to refrain from any jibes at one another. Or, as always, you can turn it over to the group to ask how they want to handle it.

Be aware that many individuals and groups are uncomfortable with conflict and will want to ignore or minimize it. If that happens, offer a "process education moment" reminding the group that the conflict has the potential to interfere with the efficiency and effectiveness of the group, and that there are positive ways to manage it.

Great Meetings!

great results

Chapter Ten

Interventions: When to Step In

EVEN WHEN YOU HAVE DONE AN EXCELLENT JOB OF ASSESSING, CONTRACTING AND SET-ting up the meeting, you will undoubtedly need to intervene in the group's process at times.

An intervention is an action by the facilitator to bring about some change in the meeting process. Interventions can be extremely subtle or can be obvious to all. For example, shifting your gaze away from a talkative member toward someone who hasn't spoken may be all that is needed to equalize participation. On the other hand, you may need to say, "I notice that many people in the room haven't spoken. How about if we hear some new voices on this question?"

> An intervention is an action by the facilitator to bring about some change in the meeting process.

The goal of intervention is to keep the meeting positive, productive, safe and on task. Therefore, the facilitator needs to alter an unproductive situation in such a way that the group is maintained and, to the fullest extent possible, so that individuals have their dignity intact and remain viable members of the group. It is also important to sort out what is distracting for you personally and what is affecting the group. For example, gum chewing may be irritating to you, but the group may not be disturbed at all. Unless the behavior keeps you from doing your job, it is not an appropriate place for an intervention.

Methods for Intervening

Disruptions to a meeting's progress can come from two sources: (1) group situations — for example, the group is tired, confused, off track, uncomfortable, dealing inappropriately with a conflict, needs a new process approach, etc.; and (2) individual behaviors of group members — for example, individuals who dominate air time, attack other group members or the facilitator, refuse to participate, etc.

Intervening in Group Situations

Here we are referring to those difficult, distracting or debilitating situations that prevent most or all of the group from accomplishing its task. The general method for intervening in a group situation is as follows:

STEP I — READ THE GROUP: Pay attention to changes in the group's energy or focus. When a usually enthusiastic group becomes silent or everyone is suddenly leaving to go to the bathroom, you are being given a message!

STEP II — CHECK WITH YOURSELF: Check to assess whether this is your issue or really a group issue. What are you feeling? Confused, tense, angry, frustrated? Where is your energy level? Is your reading of the group coming from something particular to you or is it an accurate reading of the group? The purpose of checking in with yourself is to keep from projecting personal issues onto the group. If you are exhausted from being up all night with a sick baby or are feeling lost and frustrated because of technical language the group is using, you can ask for help. However, it is important to know it's your problem, not the group's.

<u>STEP III — NAME WHAT YOU ARE PERCEIVING:</u> If necessary, interrupt the group discussion, so that you have everyone's attention. Say "Excuse me a moment" or "I'm sorry; I'm having trouble following the conversation." Then name what you are perceiving: Mirror to the group the problematic behavior you are seeing. Use descriptive, not blaming terms.

<u>STEP IV — CHECK YOUR PERCEPTION:</u> Ask the group if your interpretation of the behavior is accurate.

<u>STEP V — MAKE A RECOMMENDATION:</u> Since you are the process expert, you should offer a suggestion for how to solve the problem, rather than ask the group what to do. If the group disagrees with your idea, or has a different suggestion, by all means go with what works for the group.

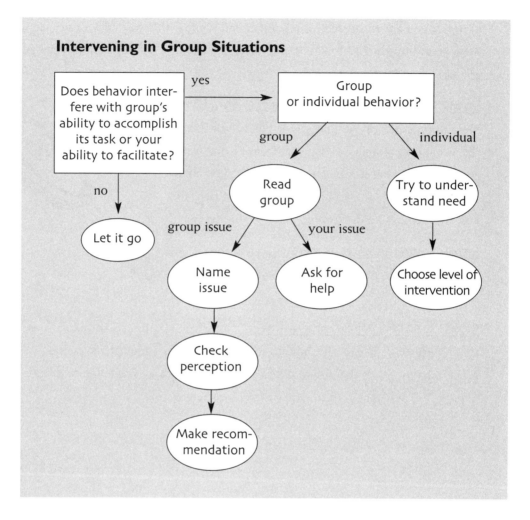

Intervening in Group Situations

Does behavior interfere with group's ability to accomplish its task or your ability to facilitate? — yes → Group or individual behavior?

no → Let it go

group → Read group

individual → Try to understand need

group issue → Name issue

your issue → Ask for help

Choose level of intervention

Name issue → Check perception → Make recommendation

Case Studies

On the following pages are three examples of group situations and possible ways to intervene. These are offered to illustrate the use of the above steps; they are not meant to be the definitive way of intervening. Please remember that there is no "cook book" method for intervention in a particular situation. Your style, the group's dynamics and its stage of development will all affect the type of intervention you choose.

Case One: The Overwhelmed Board

SITUATION: A group of ten board members has been working hard for a day and a half on a strategic plan. It is after lunch on the second and last day of this board retreat.

STEP I — READ THE GROUP: You see people looking glazed, making no eye contact with you; several people are doodling. There doesn't seem to be much energy in the room.

STEP II — CHECK WITH YOURSELF: You are a little tired but feel the work is going well and that you've been doing a good job as facilitator.

STEP III — NAME WHAT YOU ARE PERCEIVING: "I'm noticing some drooping eye lids and people's attention being elsewhere."

STEP IV — CHECK YOUR PERCEPTION: "I'm wondering if people are tired and unsure how to accomplish the rest of this task in just a few more hours?" In the discussion that follows, there is group consensus that they are feeling overwhelmed by how much work it takes to develop a strategic plan. It is clear that they won't be done by 4:00 this afternoon.

STEP V — MAKE A RECOMMENDATION: "I'd like to suggest that we stop right now and look at the big picture — identify what you've accomplished so far and what is left to be done. Then we could develop a time line for accomplishing the remainder of the plan. How does that sound?"

Case Two: Recovering From a Dramatic Incident

SITUATION: The human resources department is an hour into its monthly meeting when one of the members starts crying. She apologizes for disrupting the meeting, and tells the others that she just learned this morning that her brother has inoperable cancer.

STEP I — READ THE GROUP: You see people are frozen. Your sense of the group is that this new piece of information has surprised and saddened the group, making it unable to focus on the work at hand. A couple of people say, "Oh, I am so sorry," but otherwise there is silence. People are looking to you, apparently for guidance.

STEP II — CHECK WITH YOURSELF: You are shocked and knocked off center by what has just happened.

STEP III — NAME WHAT YOU ARE PERCEIVING: "I think we are all stunned. Mamie, what sad news."

STEP IV — CHECK YOUR PERCEPTION: In this case, you probably would want to check your perception non-verbally, making eye contact with group members, looking for nods, etc.

STEP V — MAKE A RECOMMENDATION: "I'd like to suggest we take a brief break." At this point you would go to Mamie and ask her if she would rather leave the meeting, take a few minutes as the group reconvenes to talk about her brother, or just continue the meeting. When the group reconvenes, let them know Mamie's choice. Then acknowledge that it's hard to get refocused after such news. Ask if anyone needs to say anything before you continue, and when the group is ready, proceed with the agenda.

Case Three: The Overheated Public Meeting

SITUATION: A public meeting is being held about the future of the city's biggest park. Fifty people have come out to express their opinions. Despite ground rules, the tone of the meeting is getting louder and more contentious by the minute.

STEP I — READ THE GROUP: You hear voices getting louder and louder. Speakers have started to interrupt one another. There are a lot of hands waving and people verbally expressing agreement or disagreement with a speaker.

STEP II — CHECK WITH YOURSELF: You are worried that the meeting may get out of hand. You know you have trouble with overt expression of conflict. You want to be careful not to squelch healthy conflict, but you want to establish some order.

STEP III — NAME WHAT YOU ARE PERCEIVING: Interrupt to get everyone's attention: "Excuse me, I can't hear what people are saying. Please stop talking for a moment." Stand up if necessary to get the group's attention. Then name what you are perceiving: "Many of you feel strongly about this issue and want your views heard."

STEP IV — CHECK YOUR PERCEPTION: "Let's have a show of hands to see how many people wish to have their views heard by the group."

STEP V — MAKE A RECOMMENDATION: "First, I'd like to review the ground rules and ask that you recommit yourself to them. Second, I'd like to suggest a way to proceed so that all voices get heard. It seems that we have four major groups: the neighbors of the park; those concerned about plant and animal life in the park; those who are involved in events held in the park; and those who use the park frequently. Have I missed any major groups?" If so, add them. "I'd like to suggest that we take 20 minutes and have each group come up with a list of its top five concerns and appoint one person to explain your list to the rest of us. We'll then hear from each group and end this meeting with a half hour of discussion. Does anyone have an objection to that plan?"

Intervening in Individual Non-Productive Behaviors

An intervention that is centered around one or two people calls for a slightly different approach.

STEP I: Assess the behavior and what the person's underlying need might be that gives rise to that behavior as well as the behavior's impact on the group. This doesn't mean that you have to be a psychiatrist. Remember that behaviors stem from needs, and the needs may be different from person to person. If you can understand the underlying needs of the person, you may be able to gain his productive participation in the group. Being clear about the impact on the group helps you decide which action will be most useful to the group.

STEP II: Decide what kind of intervention to make. Remember that interventions range from subtle to very obvious. Your goal is to balance empathy and understanding for the individual with the needs of the group. If the two become irreconcilable, ultimately the primary goal is to serve the group.

Interrupting Appropriately

Some of the intervention options described in this chapter require interrupting an individual who is speaking. It is hard to overcome all our childhood training that it is impolite to interrupt people, and it is important not to embarrass group participants. To interrupt effectively and compassionately remember the following points:

1. <u>LISTEN</u>: You need to listen carefully for understanding so that you can reflect back accurately the speaker's key point.

2. <u>INTERRUPT</u>: Pleasantly, but firmly interrupt saying "excuse me" and using the person's name.

3. <u>SUMMARIZE</u>: Summarize the person's key point or idea to reassure him that you understand and value his contribution.

4. <u>CHECK FOR ACCURACY</u>: Give the speaker a chance to say whether or not you understood correctly.

5. <u>CHOOSE AN APPROPRIATE ACTION</u>: For example, put the person's idea on the flipchart sheet or in the parking lot for later. Call on another person. Refer the group back to the agenda or the meeting purpose, whatever is needed.

Levels of Intervention with Individual, Non-Productive Behaviors

LEVEL ONE:

A. IGNORE BEHAVIOR, FOCUS ON CONTENT: Ignoring the difficult behavior, treat the person's core idea as a legitimate concern, using whatever summarizing or reframing is necessary. If her idea is on target for the group's current work, integrate it into their work by recording it in the appropriate place or opening discussion on it. If it is off the subject, use the parking lot to put off discussion to a later time. Often, validating a person's idea will reduce or eliminate disruptive behavior.

B. INTERRUPT, SUMMARIZE AND MOVE ON: If a participant is monopolizing the air time, follow the points above for interrupting. Summarize and capture the speaker's ideas and then move on to someone else. If someone has raised a point that is off the agenda, summarize it and get it into the parking lot or ask him to hold on to it until the appropriate part of the agenda.

> Always begin with the minimum intervention necessary to succeed, increasing the level of intervention only as required.

C. INTERRUPT, OWN THE PROBLEM AND ASK FOR HELP: If there is a distracting side conversation, rather than confronting the pair, express your own need to be able to hear better and ask for help. For example, "I'm having trouble hearing the person speaking; it would really help me if only one person talks at a time."

D. USE THE GROUND RULES: If a ground rule exists regarding side conversations, another alternative is to point to the list of ground rules to remind the group. Without naming or directly interacting with the person with the difficult behavior, she will most likely get the message.

E. <u>NAME BEHAVIOR IN GENERAL</u>: Naming the behavior in general, rather than pinning it on one person, can be effective. For example, "I'm seeing eyes rolling. Help me out — what does that mean?" If you do not get a response, you might offer your own theory on the behavior. For example, "I'm wondering if there is some concern about the amount of time this process is taking."

<u>LEVEL TWO</u>: If the behavior continues, interrupt the speaker and name the behavior. For example, "Marcus, excuse me a moment. That is the second time you have raised that concern." Check that you understand the concern: "As I wrote on the flipchart, you are afraid you will have to work overtime. Does that express your concern accurately? Is there anything you want to add?"

<u>LEVEL THREE</u>: If the behavior continues, speak to the person privately during a break or between sessions. In a friendly tone, indicate what the behavior is and what effect it is having on the group. Ask for the person's cooperation in changing the behavior.

<u>LEVEL FOUR</u>: As a last resort, if the behavior is extremely disruptive and continues, confront the person publicly. If necessary, ask the person to leave if he can't stop the behavior. This level is counterproductive both for your relationship with the person and for the cohesiveness of the group and should only be used when you are left with no other option.

Case One: Undercurrents of Hostility Between Group Members

SITUATION: You are facilitating a team meeting. There are undercurrents of hostility between Jake and Andrea. Jake rolls his eyes and sighs quietly whenever Andrea speaks. Andrea starts playing with paper clips whenever Jake speaks. You learned in your assessment that Andrea arranged to have Jake transferred from her area a couple of years ago because of personality problems. Prior to the meeting you asked each of them if they thought they could work together on this team and they both said yes.

STEP I: Assess what the behavior is and the underlying need that might give rise to that behavior. The hostility from Jake and Andrea's nervous behavior indicate that past conflicts have not been resolved.

STEP II: Decide what kind of intervention to make. Because you are unclear about how the group is being affected, you wait until the break to ask Andrea and Jake to speak with you. You decide to move to a Level Two intervention and describe the behavior you are seeing from each of them. Tell them that they need to resolve the tension between them if they are going to be contributing members of this team. You help them make a plan for resolving the tension. Then you ask that, for the remainder of this meeting, they stop their non-productive behaviors.

Case Two: The Participant Who Attacks the Facilitator

SITUATION: You are facilitating a workshop session on visioning for the VPs at the local hospital. At the beginning of the meeting, Dr. Hanes asks you what your credentials are for doing this work. She also asks if you have ever worked with hospitals before. You explain your training and experience and the role of facilitator as process, not content, expert. About an hour into the meeting, after you have suggested using the hot air balloon visioning exercise, Dr. Hanes says to you, "You don't have a clue about the reality of hospitals." And then looking at the other VPs, she says, "I question the value of continuing with this consultant."

STEP I: Assess what the behavior is and what the underlying need that might give rise to that behavior. Dr. Hanes is attacking your credibility and trying to get the other VPs to agree with her. You suspect that she is uncomfortable with the visioning process and is looking for a way to end her discomfort.

STEP II: Decide what kind of intervention to make. You start at Level One, Option E — treat it as a group concern. You say, "I hear some concern about my ability to facilitate this process. It is important that you have confidence in my ability. I'd like to hear any concerns you may have." After getting agreement from the group that you, in fact, are qualified to be their facilitator, you might need to call a break so that you can center yourself and get the meeting back on track. After the break, you talk about the challenge of, and possible discomfort in, visioning. You conduct a quick process check on the group's comfort level with what has gone on so far.

Case Three: The Nay-Sayer

SITUATION: You are in the dual role of facilitator and group member of a volunteer group which has been asked by the mayor to come up with innovative uses for a no-longer needed school building. One person, Geri, has started "yes-butting" other's ideas.

STEP I: Assess what the behavior is and what the person's underlying need might be that gives rise to that behavior. Geri is giving a reason why each idea won't work. You wonder if she is doubtful that the committee's results will be used.

STEP II: You decide to intervene on Level One, Option A: "Geri, excuse me a second. I want to make sure I understand what you are saying. You seem to feel that most of the ideas mentioned so far won't work. Do you have some thoughts about what will work?" If Geri gives some ideas, treat them respectfully and then remind everyone that in the brainstorming phase, all ideas are welcomed. If Geri says that she thinks no one will listen to the committee's ideas, poll the rest of the group for their concerns in this area, adding your own ideas at an appropriate time. Then work as a group to develop a plan for making sure your group's ideas are considered by the mayor's staff. That plan may need to be in place before the group can brainstorm with enthusiasm. If the group does not share the concern, ask Geri what she needs in order to continue to participate.

Case Four: The Dominating Speaker

<u>Situation</u>: Your work team is trying to solve a production line problem. One person, Elliot, is dominating the conversation and you are having a hard time making space for others to contribute their ideas.

>   <u>Step I</u>: Assess the behavior and the person's underlying need. Elliot is very interested in the problem and has clearly put a lot of thought into it. He has positive suggestions, but wants to elaborate on them endlessly. Elliot needs to get his ideas out and heard by the group. The other participants need some air time to get their own ideas out.

>   <u>Step II</u>: You decide to intervene on Level One, Option B, by interrupting him to summarize his thinking. You listen carefully to what he has been saying, then you interrupt him. "Elliot, excuse me, I need to interrupt you for a minute to make sure we are understanding you correctly." You summarize his points, "I believe your three suggestions are that we reroute the production line to make it accessible on both sides, invest in a new automated box closer and change the lighting over the middle section of the line." You check for accuracy. "Is that a fair summary of your ideas?" Elliot agrees that those are the key ideas. You record his ideas and simultaneously choose an appropriate action, in this case, to call on someone else. "Thank you, Elliot. I'll get those written up. Natasha, you look as if you have some ideas to share."

Intervention Steps Summary

INTERVENING IN GROUP SITUATIONS:

STEP I: Read the group

STEP II: Check with yourself

STEP III: Interrupt and reflect back

STEP IV: Check your perception

STEP V: Make a recommendation

INTERVENING IN INDIVIDUAL NON-PRODUCTIVE BEHAVIORS:

STEP I: Assess the behavior

STEP II: Choose intervention

LEVEL ONE:

A. Ignore behavior, focus on content

B. Interrupt, summarize and move on

C. Interrupt, own problem and ask for help

D. Use ground rules

E. Name behavior in general

LEVEL TWO: Interrupt and name behavior

LEVEL THREE: Speak to the person at break

LEVEL FOUR: Confront the person

Great Meetings!

great results

Chapter Eleven
Integrating Graphics Into Your Meetings

GRAPHICS REFERS TO THE VISUAL PRESENTATION OF THE GROUP'S WORK. IT IS YOUR visual way of communicating: capturing ideas, organizing and summarizing thinking, promoting clarity and understanding, and even setting a tone for the meeting. Whether you are an outside facilitator or a member of the group, your effective use of graphics will enhance the group's ability to communicate.

For example, prior to a meeting, prepare the agenda and a list of desired outcomes on large sheets. The design of those sheets and the way you organize the information will establish a sense of clarity and preparedness for the meeting.

Similarly, as you are recording information for the group and helping the group find its own understanding of issues, the use of graphics can promote clarity and understanding, add humor and organize thinking. It is important to be able to write clearly and to capture each person's idea, but using graphics can communicate concepts in a tangible way, connect ideas, and show flow or direction of actions. Graphics can serve your group in a variety of ways.

Why Use Graphics?

The following list is adapted from the work of Geoff Ball and Associates, Los Altos, CA. Using graphics can:

- help group build a shared collective view and common language
- add visual stimulation to auditory input
- reduce complex notions to relatively simple images
- show patterns of interaction and relationships
- allow people to extend their short-term memories and provide an ongoing group memory
- prevent groups from getting fixated on just one idea

Different Ways of Learning

People learn and take in information in different ways: visually, auditorily and kinesthetically. To accommodate these needs and make sure that everyone in a group is understanding clearly, you need to vary your facilitation methods and consider a variety of approaches to presenting information visually. For some, the narrative information on a list is the clearest, most understandable way to absorb information. They need to see it written down. Others may not be able to visualize from the narrative text the relationship of one activity to another, or one level of the organization to another. They may require a graphic presentation of those relationships to be able to see it. Therefore, you will want to have a number of tools at your fingertips to find the ways which help all the members of

Consider a variety of approaches to presenting information visually.

the group understand the issue at hand. Keep in mind that it may require more than one technique to reach everyone.

The nature of the group will also impact the type of graphic techniques which will be most effective. Some groups need a lot of graphic symbols to reinforce the narrative ideas on the sheet: light bulbs for new ideas or realizations; groups of little figures to underscore teams of people working together, etc. It brings the ideas to life for them. Other groups might find the symbols silly or distracting. One group might need the familiar organization of an agenda set up like a matrix with times and tasks listed in order. Others might prefer a flow chart showing the movement from one section of the agenda to another. As always, the secret is to discover the techniques that serve your group most effectively.

> The secret is to discover the techniques that serve your group most effectively.

If the group includes participants who can't see the graphic work because they are participating by phone or have a visual impairment, you will need to describe the graphics and say out loud what you are writing on the chart. It also helps to repeat what you've collected on the charts from time to time. "Let me review what we have identified so far as organizational strengths." Or, "Let me describe the umbrella image that we have used to explain the structure of the organization."

Facilitator's Supplies

Depending on the nature of your facilitation project you may need only a few supplies or a whole bag full. You may arrange for someone else to provide the basic supplies, but it is always better to be over prepared than to find yourself without something that you need. The following list will give an idea of the basic equipment.

PAPER

Flipchart Paper: There are different qualities of paper. You will need to choose the one you prefer, balancing quality and price. The paper can be plain, 1" ruled or 1" grids. Check the backing cardboard if your stand does not have a solid back to write against. Some cardboard backs are sturdier than others.

Self-Stick Paper: These flipchart size sheets have adhesive across the top and can be attached to a surface, removed, then reattached. They are easier and neater than sheets using masking tape, but are tricky to roll up at the end of the meeting. These pads are available in white and yellow.

Dry Erase Sheets: There are erasable, reusable, dry erase sheets which attach to a surface via static electricity. They come in 20" x 30" and 27" x 34". They require dry erase markers.

Butcher Paper: This sturdy white paper comes in a variety of widths up to 30" in large rolls. You will need a paper cutter or scissors to cut off the sheets. It is stronger than standard flipchart paper or newsprint and allows you to select any length you want.

Newsprint: You can contact your local newspaper for availability of the end rolls of newsprint. When available, it is generally free. The paper quality is not great, but for situations where you need a lot of paper, the price is right. In some cases, the cores will need to be returned.

MARKERS: It is important to know the difference between permanent, water based and dry erase markers. For flipchart paper, look for water based (water color) markers. You will want a large supply with a variety of colors. Permanent markers will go through the paper onto the next sheet or the wall, so it's a good idea to avoid them. For white boards, which are often found in meeting rooms, you will need dry erase markers. If you know you will be using white boards extensively, you might want to bring dry erase spray cleaner and a cloth with you. For overhead projector transparencies you will need pens which are designed for that purpose.

ELECTRONIC TOOLS

Overhead Projectors: If your group is too large to see flipcharts at the front of the room, you can use an overhead projector. You can write on the clear plastic sheets with multi-colored pens much the same way you would use a flipchart. But, when projected on the screen, more people can see it. Remember to write large enough. The down side is that when you move to the next sheet or turn the machine off your graphic record is gone from view.

Computer Projected on a Screen: There are a variety of technologies which allow you to take notes on a computer and project them onto a screen for the group to see. This gives you access to a wide array of electronic graphics. Another advantage is that you don't need to transcribe the notes after the meeting. A disadvantage is that you can't hang the group record on the wall so that you can see all the pages at once.

SCISSORS OR POCKET KNIFE: You may need to cut sheets of paper, so scissors or a pocket knife can be a useful addition to your bag of supplies.

CHALK: For working on blackboards — still available in some meeting rooms — you will want to have white and colored chalk.

TAPE: You need high quality masking tape. Cheap tape will not hold or will rip off the roll. Drafting tape is less likely to pull off paint.

SELF-STICK NOTES: The large size sticky notes (3x5 inches or larger) are useful for variations on brainstorming. You can make your own with large index cards and tape.

STARS AND DOTS: These types of stickers can be used for multivoting or at other times when you want to highlight items.

EXTRA PENS AND PAPER: It is helpful to have extra pens and paper for partici-pants to use in exercises, small group work or for taking notes.

NAME TAGS: Even if the participants know one another, name tags will help you to learn their names and to address participants personally.

BALLS, BEAN BAGS OR OTHER TOYS: A number of the warm-up exercises call for various toys such as balls and bean bags.

STANDS: If you are carrying your own stand from job to job, it needs to be portable yet sturdy. If you are looking for one which will live more permanently in a meeting room, you might want a heavier model with a solid back. Beware of plastic parts; they tend to break and are not easily replaceable.

HANDOUTS OR GRAPHIC AIDS: In some situations, it can help the group's work to have handouts. These can remind small groups in break out sessions of the questions that they are working on, or provide a grid for people to fill in during an Option Comparison Grid exercise. In design or urban planning exercises, it is helpful to have graphic aids such as maps, which participants can draw on directly or with overlays of tracing paper.

The Basics of Recording:

1. Title your pages. This helps everyone be clearer about the topic being addressed.

2. Number your pages. When it comes time to type up the group memory, you will be grateful for those numbers as you work to keep the pages of a long meeting in order.

3. Leave room in the margins and plenty of space in general. This allows you to add material later and makes for a cleaner-looking page.

4. Print, don't use script.

5. Vary the print size to EMPHASIZE an idea, but always print large enough and legibly enough to read. Experiment to find out if your writing is more legible in capital letters or small letters.

6. Separate, highlight and emphasize ideas and words with bullets, asterix, boxes, etc.

7. Use dark colored markers (black, blue, dark green, brown, purple) as the primary colors for text so everyone can see what is written. Lighter shades can be hard to read.

8. Use red, orange, pink, and other light colors for underlining, page titles, starring items, etc. Use yellow for highlighting only.

9. Alternate colors for different items — either line by line, or for different questions. It lets participants see more easily where one idea ends and the next begins.

10. Number or letter long lists — this gives people a shorthand way to refer to information: "I think #4 and #6 are saying the same thing."

11. Create a "group memory" by taping completed flipchart sheets in the order they're created to the wall so people can follow the development of information and refer back to previous discussions. Keep everything you have recorded visible to the group. This is also helpful to people who arrive after a meeting has begun. They can "read the walls" to catch up.

12. A rule of thumb is: letters should be one inch high for every ten to fifteen feet away people are from the writing.

13. Use drawings and symbols. Keep images simple: stick figures, arrows and circles, can convey a lot.

14. Give yourself permission to misspell.

15. Don't try to put too many images or words on one page — people tend to shut down when given an overload of information.

Using Graphics to Organize Thinking

An important use of graphics is to help organize the thinking of the group.

One of the most important uses of graphics is to help organize the thinking of the group by showing the relationship among ideas, statistics, activities, actions or responsibilities. The graphic possibilities can vary from a pie chart which shows the segments of a budget to a twenty foot long process plan outlining all the meetings and activities for a two year project. On the following pages are a number of formats for displaying information and organizing ideas. This is by no means a complete list, but it does illustrate a variety of possibilities.

ORGANIZATION CHART: An organization chart is among the most familiar and shows the reporting relationships within an organization. It can show succinctly who reports to whom, how many people are within a certain department or how hierarchical or horizontal the organization is.

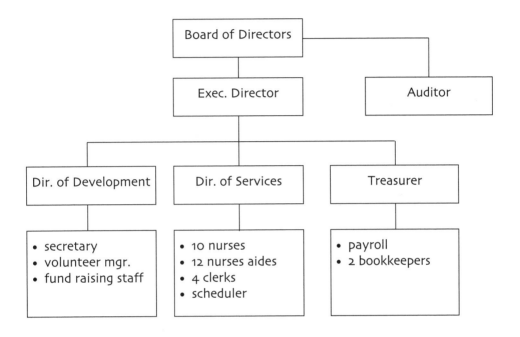

PIE CHART: A pie chart helps to show pieces of numerical information in relationship to one another and as a percentage of a whole, such as the amount of the budget spent in certain areas or the percentage of the director's time spent in certain activities.

Use of Director's Time

SOCIOGRAM: A sociogram depicts relationships within a group. It can represent subgroups whose members are very close, new members who are still isolated, and the levels of power. For example, the following group graphic shows a work team of eight people. There are three men who form one noticeable clique. One of them is the director of the department. Three other members have been on the team for some time and tend to stick together. One person doesn't seem to be a member of a group but is informally a leader. The eighth person is new and is still an outsider.

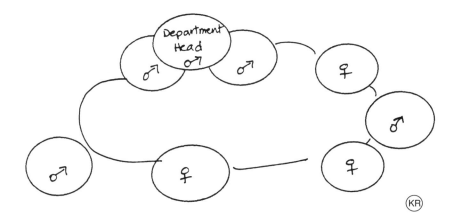

POSTER: A poster is like a billboard, condensing an idea into a visual image. It encourages people to convey the essence of something clearly, in a way that will reach other people. You can use it to do future visions, picture gallery introductions or graphic images of issues, or as a way to sum up the key learning at the end of a session. See "Picture It" in *Chapter Six: Choosing the Right Tool* and "Gallery Walk" in *Chapter Seven: Maximizing Your Group's Potential.*

BRAIN MAPPING: Brain mapping is a graphic way to display the complex ramifications of an action, or the extended subsets of an issue as they branch out from the central issue, problem or question. See "Brain Mapping" in *Chapter Six: Choosing the Right Tool.*

Implications of Layoffs

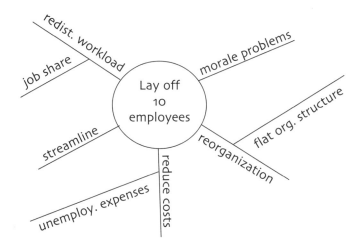

VISION MAP: A vision map is an inspiring way to show where you are, and the path leading to where you want to go. Or the map can simply show the desired future, moving from the most detailed and tangible to the most intangible aspects of the desired future.

FLOW CHART: A flow chart shows movement and direction. It is a useful way to show the steps in a process, whether a production line, an agenda, or the steps in getting a book published. A process design is a form of flow chart.

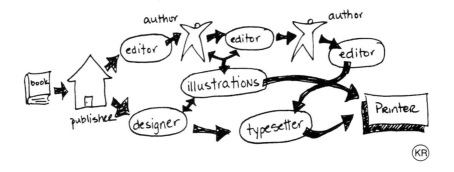

SYMBOLS AND IMAGERY: Sometimes lists of words, no matter how colorful or graphically well arranged, are just not enough to make a concept real or to effectively communicate the feeling around the idea or issue. For clarity, emotion, emphasis or humor, it can be useful to liven up your flipcharts with symbols or images which convey a message or an idea. A symbol can add a level of emotion to a concept that the printed word can seldom evoke. For example, to write "internal competition" on the list of key challenges facing your company does not evoke the same response as the graphic below.

Graphics for Your Agendas

When creating your agenda in chart form, you can use graphics to make the information more interesting, or to make a particular point. Even using color can set the tone for a more inspiring and creative meeting. If the meeting is less formal and you want to get an agenda up quickly, you can create an informal agenda using the bare minimum of details.

Another approach is a flow chart agenda, which emphasizes the movement from subject area to subject area and is made more interesting with a few graphics.

FLOW CHART AGENDA

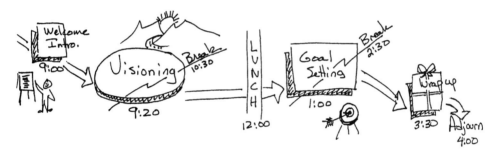

Want to add a little zest to the meeting? Try a very graphic agenda to create a sense of energy and fun.

GRAPHIC AGENDA

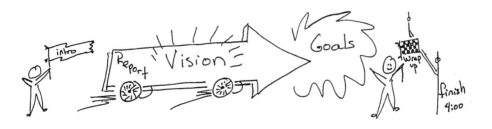

There are endless graphic possibilities, limited only by your imagination and the nature of your group. It does not require artistic talent to master a few basic shapes and forms. Stick figures, houses made of boxes and triangles, suns with big spokes of light, all the things you drew and loved as a child will do just fine. The goal is to suggest a feeling or an idea in a short lived record of a meeting, not to create museum quality art works.

Below are a few samples. Take time to practice drawing simple graphics so you have a ready reservoir when you are facilitating. Doodle away!

people

groups

partners

(KR)

expressions

sunshine   idea   t.v. media   research

board of directors   community   government

arrow   bridge   breakthrough

Great Meetings!

great results

Chapter Twelve

Reflections on the Art of Facilitation

IN THE FIRST ELEVEN CHAPTERS OF *GREAT MEETINGS! GREAT RESULTS* WE HAVE GUIDED you through the practical aspects of facilitation. We trust that, by now, you share with us the view that facilitation is an art; and like any art form, can manifest in countless ways, but is best executed with polished technical skills. Because you, the facilitator, are the instrument, the medium through which the group accomplishes its goals, we want to end by reflecting on some essential questions that every skillful, ethical facilitator should consider — and return to regularly.

Knowing Your Own Issues

Everyone has issues of his own, issues which are triggered by certain situations, particular vocabulary, types of people, or specific behaviors. Your reaction may be anger, defensiveness, withdrawal or acute discomfort. You may be reduced to tears or to the powerlessness of a child. It is not our purpose here to diagnose why these reactions arise or to resolve them. However, it is important to recognize their existence and to understand how they can affect you when you are facilitating. If you are thrown off base by a behavior which triggers one of your issues, you will have a hard time staying neutral toward that person, focusing your concentration on the task of the group or even maintaining your composure.

For example, if an older man in the group challenges your handling of the meeting and uses the same derisive phrase that your father often used and this is a lingering issue for you, it is likely to provoke a strong reaction. The reaction may be angry defensiveness or may be a complete erosion of your self-confidence, but either way it will greatly diminish your ability to serve the group.

The first step in maintaining your effectiveness in these circumstances is to identify in advance what your particular issues are likely to be and, thereby, be prepared for them. Take the time to make a list of the situations, behaviors, personality types and/or vocabulary that provoke strong reactions in you. Make your own assessment of why that might be.

Think of comments you can make to yourself to regain your balance.

Think of comments that you can make to yourself to regain your balance or to disassociate the immediate situation from the source of your emotional reaction. Be able to say to yourself, "Oh, I'm having a reaction to the phrase "bleeding heart liberal", because it feels like a put down of my own political beliefs. But I'm comfortable with my own beliefs, so I can let go of my own, personal reaction and focus on whether or not the comment needs reframing for the sake of the group." Recognition goes a long way to diffusing the intensity of your reaction.

The purpose in this discussion is not to provide a source of personal therapy, but simply to help you serve the group you are facilitating as effectively as possible by not letting your issues knock you off track.

Staying Grounded

The first part of staying grounded is to recognize and anticipate your own issues. But there are other things which can distract or disorient you while you are facilitating. It could be an angry attack directed at you or someone else in the group. It could be that you've made a mistake in choosing the process tool so that the group is bogged down — and so are you. You could simply be tired or lost yourself. Anything which affects your concentration on the group will require that you reground yourself. There are several methods you can use, depending on the nature of what is breaking your concentration.

TAKE A BREATH: Just taking a few seconds to breathe deeply will give you time to regroup. This is particularly useful when a sudden outburst or event has occurred. It gives you time to find your center or to think before you respond.

PLANT YOUR FEET: By spreading your feet a little ways apart and putting your weight evenly over them, you will literally and figuratively regain your balance when something has knocked you over.

ASK A QUESTION: If a rambling or off track comment has broken your train of thought, ask for clarification. "I'm confused. Where are you going with that thought?" Or, "I've lost track of where we are. How does your suggestion tie in?"

TAKE A BREAK: You can ask for a short break if you need a minute to reconsider the process you are using, to regain your composure or to recharge your energy. It will be time well spent if it helps you work more productively or find a better approach to the situation.

<u>TALK TO YOURSELF (SILENTLY!):</u> Identifying for yourself what is happening will help you let go of it. "I'm getting nervous because the woman in the blue shirt looks just like my fifth grade teacher who terrorized me. But she is really a different person and actually smiles very pleasantly."

Finding Your Own Definition of Success

How do you measure success when you are facilitating for a group? The purpose of using facilitation skills in designing and facilitating a meeting is to help the group to achieve the most useful or effective product that it is capable of generating. It would be a mistake to evaluate the success of your facilitation efforts by trying to decide whether or not the group's product was "good" or by taking responsibility for the content of the group's work. Instead, ask yourself if you helped the group do everything it could to generate a product that worked for them or if you helped the group work better together.

If you are working as an external facilitator, the content of the decision, solution or plan created by your group is their responsibility. You may have your own thoughts on the quality of the content or on whether or not the solution is the best one, but you are not in charge of the content. If you are comfortable that you have provided the group every opportunity to look at the question cogently, given them opportunities to generate as many creative options as possible, used techniques to make the group as productive as possible, and designed a logical, sound process, then you have been successful with that group.

If you have a dual role in the meeting and therefore have a stake in the content or result, you need to separate your evaluation of the content from your evaluation of your facilitation work. To evaluate your facilitation work, focus on questions such as:

- Did I stay neutral while I was facilitating and remember to change roles when participating?
- Did I choose tools and techniques that helped the group resolve their ques-

tions and reach the desired outcomes?

- Did I listen carefully on multiple levels and find ways for everyone to be heard?
- Did I help the group work more effectively together?

Ethical Considerations: Knowing When to Say No

The work we do in facilitation has the potential to deeply impact the lives of those with whom we work. Therefore, we believe it is of great importance to do our work with integrity. When you consider taking a facilitation assignment, there may be occasions when, for the good of the group or to take care of yourself, the best thing you can do is say no. Whether you are an outside facilitator or part of the group, it is important to consider if a facilitated meeting is appropriate or if you are the best person to facilitate. The following questions provide guidance in considering ethical and personal reasons for deciding not to facilitate:

1. IS THERE A RISK OF HARMING THE GROUP? There are situations in which a facilitated meeting will cause more harm than good. Issues may be exposed that the group is not ready to deal with. Management may already have decided not to follow through on a group's recommendations or isn't really interested in the group's input. Topics are being discussed in the wrong forum. An alert and ethical facilitator will raise these concerns during preparation for facilitation. If you believe that a facilitated meeting is not appropriate, you need to speak up. Even if you aren't skilled in knowing what should be done, trust that quiver in your stomach that this isn't a situation for facilitation.

2. WHAT ARE THE LIMITS OF MY ABILITY? Do I have the skill to facilitate this situation effectively? Are there challenges in working with the group that call for a more experienced or an outside facilitator? Whether it is lack of knowledge about the subject area (remember content literacy, not content

expertise is what you need), concern for the level of conflict in a group, or the size of the group, each of us needs to know and acknowledge our areas of strengths and weaknesses in facilitation. A facilitator should never make it harder for a group to function or accomplish its task.

3. <u>DOES ANYTHING I AM BEING ASKED TO DO COMPROMISE MY VALUES OR BELIEFS?</u> If the task of the group runs counter to your values or beliefs, then you may not want to facilitate. If the participants are being coerced into attending, or if the meeting is a thinly veiled attempt for someone to force his own agenda, consider disassociating yourself from the project. Saying no to such a project will maintain your own credibility as a person who supports healthy group process.

4. <u>IS NEUTRALITY AN ISSUE?</u> There are several aspects of neutrality to consider. The first is your own ability to be neutral. If you can't be neutral because you have strong feelings about the content of the meeting; if the facilitation involves people with such close personal ties to you that it would distort your handling of the matter; or if you have such a strong personal response to someone in the project that you don't think you can treat him objectively, then you should not facilitate. If you are a member of the group, look seriously at the line between having a stake in the outcome and feeling so strongly about supporting a particular outcome that you really want to fight for it. When you cross over that line, you should ask someone else to facilitate that meeting. The second aspect is others' perception of your neutrality. Although you may feel confident that you can be neutral in your facilitation, others may not see you as neutral. Such a perception could come from past work you have done, previous opinions that you have shared, people's perceptions about some group to which you belong or any other of a number of sources. The perception may be untrue. Nonetheless, the groups' perception is their reality. Therefore, you either need to put to rest their concerns about your neutrality or not facilitate that meeting.

5. <u>DO I HAVE ADEQUATE TIME TO PREPARE FOR AND FACILITATE THIS MEETING?</u> Time is another issue which may prompt you to say no. One of the great risks is to fill your calendar with meetings which you have agreed to facilitate, whether for hire or within your organization, and find that you have forgotten to schedule any time for the necessary preparation. Planning and design work takes time, and without it you will have difficulty serving the group well. If you can't find the time to do the preparation work, it is probably best to say no to some of the facilitation requests.

> Preparation takes time, and without it you will have difficulty serving the group well.

The bottom line in good facilitation is serving your group well. Knowing yourself, your gifts and your limits, will help you to choose those situations where you can be most effective and to serve well.

Conclusion

Facilitation is an art, not a predictable, mathematical science, nor a formula to be memorized and repeated. It is an art that we continue to perfect and improve throughout a lifetime. Hopefully, this text has given you many helpful suggestions, tools and frameworks for understanding the art of facilitation. Practicing, gaining experience, trying new ideas and observing other people at work will enrich your practical skills. Every time you work with a group you will learn something new that will impact the way you deal with the next group.

Our enthusiasm for sharing these practical suggestions for effective facilitation is based on our profound belief that bringing people together will result in a better, more thoroughly considered decision than any one of us could make on our own. Good process design and facilitation is what helps groups to succeed at the hard work of making those decisions. It enhances the quality of the result and the satisfaction of the people involved.

Most of all, remember that meetings do not have to be boring, frustrating and ineffectual. With your listening skills and attention to serving the group, your various tools and techniques, your watercolor pens and flipcharts, you can bring excitement, creativity and success to your meetings!

Great Meetings!

great results

Reading and Resources

THERE ARE MANY EXCELLENT BOOKS AND OTHER RESOURCES TO COMPLEMENT WHAT WE have written in *Great Meetings! Great Results*. Rather than try to have a comprehensive survey of the literature, we have chosen books and videos that we and our colleagues can personally recommend as helpful in facilitating or managing meetings.

Books and Pamphlets

* Bens, Ingrid, *Facilitating with Ease!*: A Step-by-Step Guidebook with Customizable Worksheets on CD-ROM, Jossey-Bass, San Francisco, CA, 2000. **www.josseybass.com**.

* BoardSource, *The Board Meeting Rescue Kit: 20 Ideas for Jumpstarting Your Board Meetings*, BoardSource, Suite 900, 1828 L. Street, NW, Washington, DC 20036-5114, 2001. **www.boardsource.org**.

- Brandt, Richard C., *Flip Charts: How to Draw Them and How to Use Them*, Jossey-Bass/Pfeiffer, San Francisco, CA, 800-274-4434, 1986. **www.josseybass.com**

- Doyle, Michael and David Straus, *How to Make Meetings Work: The New Interaction Method*, The Berkeley Publishing Group, 200 Madison, Ave., New York, NY 10016, reprint edition, 1993.

- Emery, Merrelyn and Ronald E. Purser, *The Search Conference*, Jossey Bass, San Francisco, 1996. **www.josseybass.com**

- Girsch, Maria and Charlie Girsch, *Fanning the Creative Spirit*, 2001. **www.creativitycentral.com**

- Holman, Peggy and Tom Devane, editors, *The Change Handbook: Group Methods for Shaping the Future.* Berrett-Koehler Publishers, Inc., 235 Montgomery Street, Suite 650 San Francisco, 94104-2916,1999. **www.bkconnection.com**

- Justice, Thomas and David W. Jamieson, Ph.D., *The Facilitator's Fieldbook*, American Management Association, 1601 Broadway, New York, NY 10019, 1999.

- Kaner, Sam, et al, *Facilitator's Guide to Participatory Decision Making*, New Society Publishers, 1996. **www.newsociety.com**

- Kearny, Lynn, *The Facilitator's Toolkit: Tools and Techniques for Generating Ideas and Making Decisions in Groups*, HRD Press, Amherst, MA, 1-800-822-2801, 1995.

- Owen, Harrison, *Open Space Technology: A User's Guide*, Berrett-Koehler Pub, 1998. **www.bkconnection.com**

- Rees, Fran, *Facilitator Excellence, Handbook: Helping People Work Creatively and Productively Together*, Jossey-Bass, San Francisco, 1998. **www.josseybass.com**

- Schwartz, Roger M., *The Skilled Facilitator: Practical Wisdom for Developing Effective Groups*, Jossey Bass, San Francisco, CA, 1994. **www.josseybass.com**

- Straus, David, *How to Make Collaboration Work*, Berrett-Koehler Publishers, San Francisco, 2002.**www.bkconnection.com**

- Wiesbord, Marvin, *Discovering Common Ground: How Future Search Conferences Bring People Together to Achieve Breakthrough Innovation, Empowerment, Shared Vision, and Collaborative Action*, Berrett-Koehler Publishers, 1993.**www.bkconnection.com**

- Youth on Board, *Youth on Board: Why and How to Involve Young People in Organizational Decision Making*, **www.youthonboard.org**.

Videos, DVDs and CDRoms

COMING SOON: GREAT MEETINGS! TRAINING VIDEO: This video, filmed at Eastern Kentucky University, features the authors demonstrating how to contract for a successful facilitation, conduct each phase of a meeting using various tools, and intervene in a variety of challenging situations.

COMING SOON: GREAT MEETINGS! CD ROM: The CDRom provides a chapter by chapter learning guide with exercises and quizzes, downloadable templates for tools, agenda planning sheets, etc. and short video examples of tools and good meeting practices.

Contact us at greatmeetingsinc.com or 1-888-374-6010 for more information on the video or CDRom.

AT THE TABLE: YOUTH VOICES IN DECISION MAKING – VIDEO: (2 ten minute segments) Includes discussion guide. Order from **www.youthonboard.org**

MEETINGS BLOODY MEETINGS AND MORE MEETINGS BLOODY MEETINGS: Humorous videos featuring the actor John Cleeves demonstrating how not to conduct meetings. Contact Enterprise Media LLC, 91 Harvey Street, Cambridge, MA 02140, 1-800-423-6021 for free preview or information on rental or purchase.

STARTING MEETINGS SUCCESSFULLY: SET UP YOUR NEXT MEETING FOR SUCCESS: featuring David Sibbet. This video demonstrates, with graphics, how to use the OARRS model for meeting openers. This and several other videos, as well as facilitator supplies, are available at **www.grove.com/store**.

Great Meetings!

great results

Index

Great Meetings!

great results

About the Authors

Pam Plumb (left) and Dee Kelsey

DEE KELSEY AND PAM PLUMB BEGAN THEIR COLLA-boration when they created the Certificate Program in Facilitation for the Center for Continuing Education at the University of Southern Maine in 1993. Since then, they have designed and delivered customized facilitation and meeting management training programs for clients as varied as L.L. Bean, The National League of Cities, Bates College, Eastern Kentucky University and The Nature Conservancy. Dee and Pam are currently putting the final touches on *Great Meetings! The Training Video* and *Great Meetings! The CD Rom.* (See *Reading and Resources* for details.)

Dee has worked both as a trainer and personnel representative at Hewlett Packard and as a mediator for the city of Palo Alto, California. After completing her Masters in Intercultural Management, she returned to Maine. Since 1985, as principal of Dee Kelsey and Associates, Dee has provided organizational development, facilitation, process consultation, mediation, and training services to hundreds of clients ranging from small work groups to large corporations.

Pam Plumb discovered during her years as a City Councilor and Mayor of Portland that effective meeting planning and facilitation made a big difference in meeting outcomes. In 1991, she created Pamela Plumb & Associates which serves a wide range of non-profit organizations, businesses and government organizations with process design, facilitation, training and organizational development.

About Great Meetings, Inc.

Great Meetings! Inc. not only publishes *Great Meetings! Great Results*, but will soon be offering the *Great Meetings! The Training Video*. This production features the authors demonstrating how to contract for a successful facilitation, conduct each phase of a meeting and intervene in a variety of challenging situations. Additionally, *Great Meetings! CD Rom* is in production. The CD provides a chapter by chapter learning guide with exercises and quizzes, downloadable templates for tools, agenda planning sheets, etc., and short video examples of tools and good meeting practices. Additional future products will include training workbooks, a trainer's manual and train-the-trainer courses.